Level G

MATHEMATICS

Skills, Concepts, Problem Solving

Author: Albert E. Filano

Editor: K. E. Possler

Illustrator: Jack Kershner

Cover Illustrator: Cary Michael Trout

ISBN 0-8454-0177-7

Continental Press

Elizabethtown, PA 17022

Contents

3	Place Value: Through Hundred Thousands
4	Place Value: Millions and Billions
5	Comparing and Ordering Numbers
6	Rounding Numbers
7	Properties of Addition
8	Subtraction: Basic Facts
9	Adding Whole Numbers
10	Subtracting Whole Numbers
11	Subtracting Across Zeros
12	Problem Solving: Choosing the Operation
13	Addition and Subtraction Practice
14	Estimating Sums and Differences
15	Problem Solving: Using Estimation
16	Problem Solving: Using a Check Register
17	Properties of Multiplication
18	Multiplying by One-Digit Numbers
19	Problem Solving: Writing an Equation
20	Division with Remainders
21	Problem Solving: Interpreting a Remainder
22	Dividing by One-Digit Numbers
23	Dividing Larger Numbers
24	Problem Solving: Planning Multiple-Step Solutions
25	Order of Operations
26	Multiplying by Tens, Hundreds, or Thousands
27	Multiplying by Two-Digit Numbers
28	Multiplying by Three-Digit Numbers
29	Problem Solving: Identifying Extra Information
30	Estimating Products
31	Dividing by Tens
32	Dividing by Two-Digit Numbers
33	Dividing by Three-Digit Numbers
34	Problem Solving: Identifying Insufficient Information
35	Estimating Quotients
36	Problem Solving: Completing a Table
37	Least Common Multiple
38	Greatest Common Factor
39	Prime and Composite Numbers
40	Rules of Divisibility
41	Problem Solving: Guessing and Checking
42	Equivalent Fractions
43	Simplifying Fractions
44	Adding Fractions
45	Subtracting Fractions
46	Problem Solving: Using Fractions
47	Mixed Numbers and Fractions
48	Comparing and Ordering Fractions and Mixed Numbers
49	Adding Mixed Numbers
50	Subtracting Mixed Numbers
51	Problem Solving: Using Mixed Numbers
52	Multiplying Fractions
53	Multiplying Fractions and Whole Numbers
54	Multiplying Mixed Numbers
55	Reciprocals and Dividing by Fractions
56	Dividing Fractions
57	Dividing Mixed Numbers
58	Problem Solving: Using the Four Operations with Fractions
59	Decimals: Place Value
60	Comparing and Ordering Decimals
61	Adding Decimals
62	Subtracting Decimals
63	Rounding Decimals
64	Estimating Decimal Sums and Differences
65	Problem Solving: Using Decimals
66	Multiplying and Dividing Decimals by 10; 100; 1,000
67	Multiplying Decimals
68	Dividing Decimals by Whole Numbers
69	Dividing Decimals by Decimals
70	Dividing Decimals: Annexing Zeros
71	Estimating Decimal Products and Quotients
72	Problem Solving: Using the Four Operations with Decimals
73	Problem Solving: Finding Elapsed Time
74	Measurement: Metric Units of Length
75	Measurement: Metric Units of Capacity and Mass
76	Measurement: Customary Units of Length
77	Measurement: Customary Units of Capacity and Weight
78	Problem Solving: Using Hidden Information
79	Ratios
80	Proportions
81	Problem Solving: Using Proportions
82	Fractions, Decimals, and Percents
83	Finding a Percent of a Number
84	Finding a Percent
85	Finding Discount and Sales Tax
86	Problem Solving: Using Percents
87	Geometry: Basic Concepts
88	Geometry: Measuring Angles
89	Geometry: Classifying Angles
90	Geometry: Parallel and Intersecting Lines
91	Geometry: Triangles
92	Geometry: Quadrilaterals
93	Geometry: Congruent and Similar Polygons
94	Geometry: Symmetry
95	Geometry: Translations, Rotations, and Reflections
96	Geometry: Circles
97	Geometry: Perimeter
98	Geometry: Circumference
99	Geometry: Area of Rectangles and Parallelograms
100	Geometry: Area of Triangles
101	Geometry: Area of Circles
102	Geometry: Solid Figures
103	Geometry: Surface Area
104	Geometry: Volume
105	Problem Solving: Using Formulas
106	Interpreting Data
107	Reading Double-Bar Graphs
108	Reading and Making Line Graphs
109	Problem Solving: Using a Circle Graph
110	Problem Solving: Making a Tree Diagram
111	Probability
112	Certainty and Impossibility
113	Probability of Independent Events
114	Introduction to Integers
115	Comparing and Ordering Integers
116	Adding Integers
117	Subtracting Integers
118	Adding and Subtracting Integers Practice
119	Problem Solving: Using Integers
120	Ordered Pairs

ALASKA
589,757
square miles

Alaska, our largest state, has an area of five hundred eighty-nine thousand, seven hundred fifty-seven square miles.

Write each number in standard form.

1. eighty-five _____

2. two hundred nine _____

3. four hundred sixteen _____

4. three thousand, ninety-two _____

5. six thousand, three hundred _____

6. fifty-four thousand, seven hundred eight _____

7. two hundred thirty-eight thousand, six hundred ten _____

8. seven hundred five thousand, nine hundred forty-three _____

Write the total value of each underlined digit.

9. 6̲2 _____

10. 1̲50 _____

11. 7,6̲28 _____

12. 2̲3,506 _____

13. 5̲0,041 _____

14. 9̲80,200 _____

Below are some facts about the United States. For each number, write a number name. For each number name, write a number in standard form.

15. The smallest state, Rhode Island, has an area of 1,214 square miles.

_____

16. Our tallest peak is Mount McKinley, which is twenty thousand, three hundred twenty feet tall. _____

17. The United States has about 78,267 square miles of inland waters.

_____

18. From its source to its mouth, the Mississippi River stretches three thousand, seven hundred ten miles. _____

19. The largest state has a small population, only 550,000 people.

_____

20. When our country was new, its entire area was only eight hundred sixty-four thousand, seven hundred forty-six square miles. _____

Place Value: Through Hundred Thousands

The orbit of the planet Pluto takes it 4 billion, 551 million, 4 hundred thousand miles from the sun.

billions

4,551,400,000 miles

millions

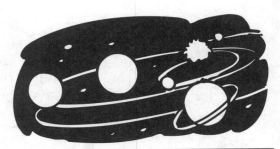

Write each number in standard form.

1. nine hundred ninety-nine thousand, nine hundred ninety-nine _____

2. six million _____

3. two billion _____

4. eighty million, six hundred fifty-one thousand _____

5. four billion, one hundred million, five hundred thousand _____

6. six hundred billion, seven hundred twenty-five million _____

7. seventy-six billion, eight hundred thousand, fifteen _____

Write the number that tells how many.

8. 4,180,390 _____180_____ thousands

9. 7,205,614,000 _____ millions

10. 803,920,700,110 _____ billions

11. 50,108,600,425 _____ millions

12. 893,276,019,000 _____ billions

13. 209,006,900,003 _____ millions

14. 47,000,090,000 _____ thousands

15. 14,563,298 _____ millions

Use the table to answer each question.

DISTANCE FROM SUN IN MILES		
Planet	**Maximum**	**Minimum**
Mercury	43,400,000	28,600,000
Venus	67,700,000	66,800,000
Earth	94,600,000	91,400,000
Mars	155,000,000	128,500,000
Jupiter	507,000,000	460,600,000
Saturn	937,500,000	838,400,000
Uranus	1,859,700,000	1,669,300,000
Neptune	2,821,700,000	2,760,400,000
Pluto	4,551,400,000	2,756,400,000

16. How close does Mercury get to the sun? _____

17. How far does Mars get from the sun? _____

18. Which planet orbits the sun at a distance of about 500 million miles?

_____

19. Which planets orbit less than 100 million miles from the sun? _____

_____

20. Which planets orbit more than 1 billion miles from the sun? _____

_____

The symbol > means *is greater than*. The symbol < means *is less than*. To compare two numbers, compare the digits in like places, beginning on the left.

$$27,613 > 27,524 \qquad 939,999 < 940,700$$

Notice that the symbol always points to the smaller number.

Write > or < in each circle.

1. 287 ◯ 278
2. 71,546 ◯ 72,545
3. 5,000,000 ◯ 672,000

4. 904 ◯ 913
5. 13,821 ◯ 1,482
6. 2,864,150 ◯ 2,784,149

7. 6,510 ◯ 6,482
8. 406,934 ◯ 406,843
9. 6,386,271 ◯ 6,394,270

10. 3,052 ◯ 2,953
11. 762,501 ◯ 763,400
12. 80,000,000 ◯ 8,957,929

The table on the right shows the five states with the greatest populations in 1997. Write number sentences using > and < to compare the populations of the states listed below.

State	Population
California	31,431,000
Florida	13,953,000
New York	18,169,000
Pennsylvania	12,052,000
Texas	18,378,000

13. New York / Texas _____ ◯ _____

14. Pennsylvania / California _____ ◯ _____

15. Florida / New York _____ ◯ _____

16. Texas / Pennsylvania _____ ◯ _____

17. California / Texas _____ ◯ _____

18. New York / California _____ ◯ _____

19. Pennsylvania / Florida _____ ◯ _____

List the names of the states in order of their size, beginning with the largest.

20. _____

21. _____

22. _____

23. _____

24. _____

Round a number to any place by looking at the next digit on the **right**. If that digit is 4 or less, round **down**. If that digit is 5 or more, round **up**.

Round to the nearest **thousand** by looking at the **hundreds**.

75,901,342 → 75,901,000

Round to the nearest **million** by looking at the **hundred thousands**.

75,901,342 → 76,000,000

Listed below are some football stadiums and the number of people each one holds. Round the capacity of each stadium to the nearest ten, hundred, and thousand.

	Stadium	Capacity	Ten	Hundred	Thousand
1.	Veterans	64,899			
2.	Silverdome	80,368			
3.	Astrodome	59,969			
4.	Carolinas	72,500			
5.	Mile High	76,273			
6.	Foxboro	60,292			
7.	R.F. Kennedy	56,454			
8.	Louisiana Superdome	69,056			
9.	San Diego	60,794			
10.	Texas	65,812			

Listed below are the populations of the United States in various years. Round each figure to the nearest thousand and million.

	Year	Population	Thousand	Million
11.	1980	226,504,825		
12.	1950	151,325,798		
13.	1900	75,994,575		
14.	1850	23,191,876		
15.	1800	5,308,483		

COMMUTATIVE PROPERTY	IDENTITY PROPERTY	ASSOCIATIVE PROPERTY
9 + 6 = 6 + 9	8 + 0 = 8	(3 + 5) + 6 = 3 + (5 + 6)
You can add numbers in any order. The sum remains the same.	When you add 0 to a number, the sum is the other number.	You can group numbers in any way. The sum remains the same.

Write the name of the property that each equation illustrates.

1. 7 + (9 + 1) = (7 + 9) + 1 _____

2. 3 + 0 = 3 _____

3. 5 + 8 = 8 + 5 _____

4. (6 + 2) + 4 = 6 + (2 + 4) _____

5. 7 + 6 = 6 + 7 _____

6. 9 + 0 = 0 + 9 _____

Write the number that makes each equation true.

7. 5 + 8 = _____ + 5

8. 4 + 0 = _____

9. (3 + 4) + 7 = _____ +7

10. 9 + 8 = 8 + _____

11. 2 + (6 + 7) = 2 + _____

12. (5 + 2) + 8 = _____ + 8

13. 4 + 7 = 7 + _____

14. 0 + 8 = _____

15. (1 + 9) + 6 = 10 + _____

16. 8 + 7 = 7 + _____

17. 5 + (8 + 8) = 5 + _____

18. 9 + (5 + 6) = 9 + _____

Find the total score for each dart board below. Use the scores with darts. Circle the highest score and mark the lowest score with an X.

19.

Score = _____

20.

Score = _____

21.
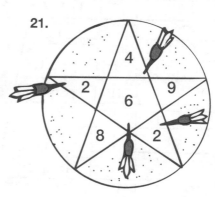

Score = _____

Subtraction is the inverse of addition.
For example, $14 - 6 = 8$ because $6 + 8 = 14$.
You can think of addition to help you subtract.

Subtract. Think of addition.

1. $\begin{array}{r} 10 \\ -2 \\ \hline \end{array}$
2. $\begin{array}{r} 14 \\ -7 \\ \hline \end{array}$
3. $\begin{array}{r} 15 \\ -9 \\ \hline \end{array}$
4. $\begin{array}{r} 11 \\ -8 \\ \hline \end{array}$
5. $\begin{array}{r} 13 \\ -5 \\ \hline \end{array}$
6. $\begin{array}{r} 12 \\ -3 \\ \hline \end{array}$

7. $\begin{array}{r} 16 \\ -9 \\ \hline \end{array}$
8. $\begin{array}{r} 10 \\ -6 \\ \hline \end{array}$
9. $\begin{array}{r} 18 \\ -9 \\ \hline \end{array}$
10. $\begin{array}{r} 14 \\ -5 \\ \hline \end{array}$
11. $\begin{array}{r} 13 \\ -7 \\ \hline \end{array}$
12. $\begin{array}{r} 11 \\ -5 \\ \hline \end{array}$

13. $\begin{array}{r} 12 \\ -8 \\ \hline \end{array}$
14. $\begin{array}{r} 17 \\ -9 \\ \hline \end{array}$
15. $\begin{array}{r} 11 \\ -4 \\ \hline \end{array}$
16. $\begin{array}{r} 15 \\ -7 \\ \hline \end{array}$
17. $\begin{array}{r} 10 \\ -5 \\ \hline \end{array}$
18. $\begin{array}{r} 12 \\ -4 \\ \hline \end{array}$

19. $\begin{array}{r} 17 \\ -8 \\ \hline \end{array}$
20. $\begin{array}{r} 15 \\ -6 \\ \hline \end{array}$
21. $\begin{array}{r} 14 \\ -9 \\ \hline \end{array}$
22. $\begin{array}{r} 16 \\ -8 \\ \hline \end{array}$
23. $\begin{array}{r} 13 \\ -4 \\ \hline \end{array}$
24. $\begin{array}{r} 12 \\ -5 \\ \hline \end{array}$

Use the facts in the illustration below to solve each problem.

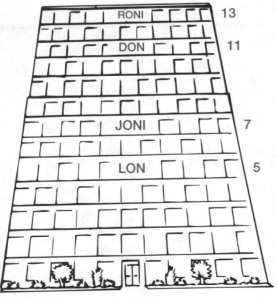

RONI — 13
DON — 11
JONI — 7
LON — 5

25. How many floors below
    Don does Joni live?

_____

26. How many floors does
    Roni live above Lon?

_____

27. Roni walked down 7 floors
    to visit a friend. On which
    floor did her friend live?

Subtraction: Basic Facts

```
  1
  28
+ 37
  65
```
Regroup 15 ones as 1 ten and 5 ones.

Sometimes you must regroup more than once.

```
  1 1
  465
+ 167
  632
```

```
  1 1 1 1
  43,678
+ 28,449
  72,127
```

Add.

1.
```
  54
+ 32
```

2.
```
  16
+ 74
```

3.
```
  28
+ 28
```

4.
```
  39
+ 43
```

5.
```
  46
+ 18
```

6.
```
  862
+ 109
```

7.
```
  355
+ 374
```

8.
```
  269
+ 639
```

9.
```
  153
+  78
```

10.
```
  229
+ 596
```

11.
```
  $18.46
+ 44.69
```

12.
```
  $64.79
+ 28.58
```

13.
```
  $39.65
+ 37.75
```

14.
```
  $80.72
+  9.49
```

15.
```
  23,904
  17,568
+ 20,504
```

16.
```
  27,187
  23,859
+ 24,651
```

17.
```
  603,486
   49,925
+ 212,438
```

18.
```
  517,363
  199,957
+ 113,574
```

Use the table to find the total cost of each purchase below.

SURFSTAR List Price	
Standard Model	$ 9,047.19
Deluxe Z-Series	12,478.25
Air Conditioning	721.76
Safety Package	575.18
Stereo Radio	328.97

19. the deluxe Z-series Surfstar with air conditioning

_____

20. the standard model Surfstar with the safety package

_____

21. the standard model Surfstar with the safety package, the stereo radio, and air conditioning

$$\begin{array}{r} \scriptstyle 3\ 12 \\ \cancel{4}\cancel{2} \\ -1\ 6 \\ \hline 2\ 6 \end{array}$$

Regroup 4 tens as 3 tens and 10 ones.

Regroup as many times as you need to.

$$\begin{array}{r} \scriptstyle 16 \\ \scriptstyle 1\ \cancel{8}\ 15 \\ \cancel{2}\cancel{7}\cancel{5} \\ -1\ 8\ 6 \\ \hline 8\ 9 \end{array}$$

$$\begin{array}{r} \scriptstyle 11 \\ \scriptstyle 4\ \cancel{1}\ 14\ 2\ 11 \\ \cancel{5}\cancel{2},\cancel{4}\cancel{3}\cancel{1} \\ -2\ 5,8\ 1\ 9 \\ \hline 2\ 6,6\ 1\ 2 \end{array}$$

Subtract.

1. $\begin{array}{r} 67 \\ -39 \\ \hline \end{array}$
2. $\begin{array}{r} 35 \\ -17 \\ \hline \end{array}$
3. $\begin{array}{r} 28 \\ -\ 9 \\ \hline \end{array}$
4. $\begin{array}{r} 81 \\ -25 \\ \hline \end{array}$
5. $\begin{array}{r} 92 \\ -16 \\ \hline \end{array}$

6. $\begin{array}{r} 325 \\ -129 \\ \hline \end{array}$
7. $\begin{array}{r} 624 \\ -257 \\ \hline \end{array}$
8. $\begin{array}{r} 579 \\ -380 \\ \hline \end{array}$
9. $\begin{array}{r} 928 \\ -425 \\ \hline \end{array}$
10. $\begin{array}{r} 761 \\ -595 \\ \hline \end{array}$

11. $\begin{array}{r} \$41.43 \\ -16.25 \\ \hline \end{array}$
12. $\begin{array}{r} \$79.29 \\ -29.78 \\ \hline \end{array}$
13. $\begin{array}{r} \$86.31 \\ -40.74 \\ \hline \end{array}$
14. $\begin{array}{r} \$52.43 \\ -39.16 \\ \hline \end{array}$

15. $\begin{array}{r} 92,658 \\ -57,899 \\ \hline \end{array}$
16. $\begin{array}{r} 30,352 \\ -10,306 \\ \hline \end{array}$
17. $\begin{array}{r} 617,923 \\ -409,457 \\ \hline \end{array}$
18. $\begin{array}{r} 713,478 \\ -230,912 \\ \hline \end{array}$

Use the advertisement to solve each problem.

HOME OFFICE WORKS
Annual Sale!

MBI Computer
Regularly $1,955.95
Now $1,299.99

Super Laser Printer
Was $1,425.50
Now $1,275.99

FAX Machine
Was $819.16
Now $345.95!

19. How much less does the computer cost on sale than it does regularly?

20. How much less than usual does the FAX machine cost on sale?

21. How much greater is the regular price of the laser printer than the regular price of the FAX machine?

Subtracting Whole Numbers

$$\begin{array}{r} \overset{9}{\cancel{1}}\overset{}{\cancel{1}}013 \\ \cancel{2}\cancel{0}\cancel{3} \\ -129 \\ \hline 74 \end{array}$$

$$\begin{array}{r} \overset{9}{}\overset{9}{} \\ 4\ \cancel{1}\cancel{0}\cancel{1}\cancel{0}10 \\ \cancel{5},\cancel{0}\cancel{0}\cancel{0} \\ -2,355 \\ \hline 2,645 \end{array}$$

$$\begin{array}{r} \overset{10}{} \\ 8\ \cancel{0}\ 12 \\ \cancel{9},\cancel{1}\cancel{2}5 \\ -2,560 \\ \hline 6,565 \end{array}$$

You can't subtract from zero. Take 1 from the next place on the left and regroup it for the zero.

Subtract.

1.
$$\begin{array}{r} 300 \\ -197 \\ \hline \end{array}$$

2.
$$\begin{array}{r} 514 \\ -228 \\ \hline \end{array}$$

3.
$$\begin{array}{r} 607 \\ -591 \\ \hline \end{array}$$

4.
$$\begin{array}{r} 800 \\ -372 \\ \hline \end{array}$$

5.
$$\begin{array}{r} 911 \\ -483 \\ \hline \end{array}$$

6.
$$\begin{array}{r} 1,000 \\ -\ \ 636 \\ \hline \end{array}$$

7.
$$\begin{array}{r} 4,028 \\ -1,755 \\ \hline \end{array}$$

8.
$$\begin{array}{r} 7,006 \\ -5,824 \\ \hline \end{array}$$

9.
$$\begin{array}{r} 2,300 \\ -1,189 \\ \hline \end{array}$$

10.
$$\begin{array}{r} 5,000 \\ -2,007 \\ \hline \end{array}$$

11.
$$\begin{array}{r} \$20.00 \\ -10.98 \\ \hline \end{array}$$

12.
$$\begin{array}{r} \$40.50 \\ -25.70 \\ \hline \end{array}$$

13.
$$\begin{array}{r} \$91.00 \\ -79.15 \\ \hline \end{array}$$

14.
$$\begin{array}{r} \$30.00 \\ -12.08 \\ \hline \end{array}$$

15.
$$\begin{array}{r} 40,000 \\ -23,561 \\ \hline \end{array}$$

16.
$$\begin{array}{r} 80,702 \\ -\ 1,509 \\ \hline \end{array}$$

17.
$$\begin{array}{r} 100,986 \\ -\ 25,214 \\ \hline \end{array}$$

18.
$$\begin{array}{r} 704,000 \\ -431,098 \\ \hline \end{array}$$

Use the table to solve each problem.

ISLAND NATION	AREA IN SQUARE KILOMETERS
Cuba	114,524
Cyprus	9,251
Iceland	103,000
Madagascar	587,041
Sri Lanka	65,610

19. What is the difference in size between the largest and smallest islands?

20. How much larger is Iceland than Cyprus?

21. How much smaller is Cuba than Madagascar?

Subtracting Across Zeros

11

Use these four steps to find answers to the problems below.

Step 1. **Read** the problem carefully.

Step 2. **Think:** What do I know?
What must I find out?
What operations should I use?

Step 3. **Solve:** Write the problem and find the answer.

Step 4. **Check** the answer. Does it make sense?

1. Sofia counted 13 swans, 118 ducks, 81 geese, and 136 shorebirds in one day at a wildlife preserve. How many birds did she count in all?

2. How many more geese than swans did Sofia count?

3. Drew counted 289 birds at the preserve. How many more or fewer birds was that than Sofia counted?

4. In North America, 836 kinds of birds can be seen. The most any one person has seen is 745 kinds. How many has that person not seen?

5. Drew began birding this year and has seen 82 kinds of birds. If he wants to see North American birds, how many more kinds can he see?

6. This year, 329 birds were banded in August, 1,009 in September, 2,117 in October, and 985 in November. How many were banded in those four months?

7. Last year, 4,203 birds were banded. How many more or fewer birds is that than this year?

8. An arctic tern migrated 35,400 kilometers from the Arctic to the Antarctic. Then it flew back to the Arctic. How long was the entire trip?

Problem Solving: Choosing the Operation

Add or subtract. Watch the signs.

1. 418
    +497

2. 9,356
    −5,289

3. 15,007
    +86,926

4. 90,000
    −41,034

5. 356,914
    +697,576

6. 760
    −364

7. 4,270
    +3,599

8. 27,534
    +37,649

9. 51,003
    − 9,359

10. 804,601
    −260,299

Write the correct digit in each blank to complete the problems. Check your answers.

11. _ _ _
     +564
     862

12. 842
     −_ _ _
     675

13. _39
     +2_5
     70_

14. 6_5
     −29_
     _77

15. 3_6
     +_8_
     542

16. 9,_42
     −_,5_5
     5,45_

17. 3,76_
     +4,_68
     _,3_2

18. _2,_1_
     −17,994
     4_,0_1

19. 8_6,4_3
     +_00,_71
     92_,004

Write the correct sign, + or −. Then complete each problem. Check your answers.

20. 71_
     3_4
     346

21. 2,_8_
     _,1_9
     5,930

22. _5,_8_
     4_,3_6
     80,000

23. 7_1,812
     _43,_1_
     108,001

Find the missing digits to complete the statements below.

24. The library owns _2,74_ books. An
    average of 3_,_95 books are in circulation
    at any time. That means there are usually
    around 61,8_0 books on the shelves.

25. The local government provided $27_,90_
    to run the library. The library also received
    $_2,608 in donations. So the library had
    $_18,_08 to operate.

Addition and Subtraction Practice

13

Estimate sums and differences by rounding the numbers.

```
  295
  508
+ 186
```

300 plus 500 plus 200 is 1,000. So the answer is about 1,000.

```
 $52.25
- 18.75
```

$50.00 minus $20.00 is $30.00. So the answer is about $30.00.

Estimate each answer. Then solve and compare the estimated and exact answers.

1.
```
   87
   62
+  33
```
about

_____

2.
```
  $3.19
   2.96
+  4.87
```
about

_____

3.
```
  $2.88
   4.92
+  1.07
```
about

_____

4.
```
  7,142
- 2,058
```
about

_____

5.
```
  6,083
- 1,987
```
about

_____

6.
```
  8,871
- 5,965
```
about

_____

7.
```
  $51.79
+  38.23
```
about

_____

8.
```
  50,340
- 19,508
```
about

_____

9.
```
  $48.75
+  29.98
```
about

_____

10.
```
  82,125
- 43,076
```
about

_____

11.
```
  94,002
- 72,850
```
about

_____

12.
```
  28,240
+ 61,968
```
about

_____

Use the chart to find the estimated and exact answers for each problem.

Sales-person	Miles Traveled	
	Last Year	This Year
Joan	19,150	21,375
Cole	10,245	9,960

13. How many miles did Joan and Cole travel this year?

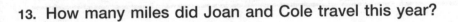

14. How many more miles did Joan drive than Cole last year?

Estimating Sums and Differences

For some problems an exact answer is not needed.

SUMMER SPECIALS AT SUPER SAVER CENTER!

Contact lens cleaner	$5.90	Itch-Away lotion	$3.79	Motion-sickness	
Contact lens wetting		Bug-Off spray	$4.82	pills	$7.14
solution	$6.45	One-Time flea bomb	$5.33	Dry-Up Allergy	
Eye-Soother drops	$2.49	Katz flea collars	$2.77	capsules	$6.99
Designer sunglasses	$12.15	Stomach Soother		First-aid kit	$14.17
Super Sun Block	$4.01	tablets	$1.49	Antiseptic spray	$3.15
Sunburn spray	$2.66	Aspirin	$.89	Adhesive bandages	$1.52

Use estimates and the newspaper advertisement above to answer each question.

1. Marcia has $20.00. She needs to buy some Super Sun Block and would like a pair of designer sunglasses. Does she have enough money for both?

2. Jafar sometimes gets seasick on boats. He wants to buy motion-sickness pills and some Stomach Soother tablets. Will $8.00 be enough for both?

3. Mr. Lavorini wants to buy flea collars for his two cats and a One-Time flea bomb. Is $15.00 enough to pay for these things?

4. Eulalia wants to buy contact lens cleaner and contact lens wetting solution. If she has $14.79, can she afford them?

5. Trung Ky needs sunburn spray, Itch-Away lotion, and aspirin. Should he expect to spend more than $8.00?

6. Mrs. Jenkins bought a first-aid kit, some antiseptic spray, and adhesive bandages. Did she spend more than $20.00?

7. Lenora needs a pack of Dry-Up Allergy capsules and a bottle of Eye-Soother drops. She has $10.00. Does she have enough money?

8. Blake has $21.37. He has to buy a can of Bug-Off spray and a first-aid kit for his camping trip. Will he have enough left for aspirin?

A **check register** shows how much money is in a checking account.
A **payment** is money taken out. It is subtracted from the **balance**.
A **deposit** is money put in. It is added to the balance.

Find the new balance after each payment and deposit in the registers below. Be sure to check your work.

No.	Description of Transaction	Payment	Deposit	Balance
		$	$	$ 602 74
	Mrs. Yokama - lawn		15 00	
	Mrs. Fleischer - washing car		18 50	
206	Dr. Max Cohen	54 00		
207	Tune Time Records	18 39		
208	guitar lesson	29 00		
	Sullivan - odd jobs		45 00	
209	Veletto's Department Store	152 75		

No.	Description of Transaction	Payment	Deposit	Balance
				$ 1,562 70
101	McCullogh's Garage	$108 45	$	
102	Eatright Market	56 92		
	pay check		265 22	
103	Jeans Scene	19 08		
	Pablo Rodriguez		25 00	
104	Shutterbug Shop	5 85		
105	Dr. Birnbaum	38 00		

Problem Solving: Using a Check Register

COMMUTATIVE PROPERTY $6 \times 7 = 7 \times 6$	You can multiply factors in any order. The product remains the same.
IDENTITY PROPERTY $1 \times 8 = 8$	If one of the factors is 1, the product is the other factor.
PROPERTY OF ZERO $9 \times 0 = 0$	If one of the factors is 0, the product is 0.
ASSOCIATIVE PROPERTY $(3 \times 2) \times 4 = 3 \times (2 \times 4)$	You can group factors in any way. The product remains the same.
DISTRIBUTIVE PROPERTY $2 \times (3 + 5) = (2 \times 3) + (2 \times 5)$	To multiply the sum of two numbers, multiply each addend by the factor and then add the products.

Write the name of the property each equation illustrates.

1. $8 \times 9 = 9 \times 8$ _____

2. $(2 \times 4) \times 5 = 2 \times (4 \times 5)$ _____

3. $0 \times 5 = 0$ _____

4. $5 \times (4 + 3) = (5 \times 4) + (5 \times 3)$ _____

5. $6 \times (8 \times 2) = (6 \times 8) \times 2$ _____

6. $7 \times 1 = 7$ _____

7. $2 \times (4 + 9) = (2 \times 4) + (2 \times 9)$ _____

8. $7 \times 5 = 5 \times 7$ _____

Write the number that makes each equation true.

9. $5 \times 1 = $ _____

10. $(3 \times 6) \times 7 = 3 \times ($ _____ $\times 7)$

11. $9 \times 0 = $ _____

12. $5 \times 3 = $ _____ $\times 5$

13. $9 \times (3 + 2) = (9 \times 3) + ($ _____ $\times 2)$

14. $2 \times (3 \times 2) = 2 \times$ _____

15. $5 \times (5 + 1) = 5 \times$ _____

16. $7 \times (6 + 3) = (6 + 3) \times$ _____

Properties of Multiplication

$$
\begin{array}{r}
{}^{6} \\
78 \\
\times 8 \\
\hline
624
\end{array}
\qquad
\begin{array}{r}
{}^{2} \\
251 \\
\times 4 \\
\hline
1,004
\end{array}
\qquad
\begin{array}{r}
{}^{1}{}^{1} \\
2,716 \\
\times 2 \\
\hline
5,432
\end{array}
$$

Multiply each place, starting on the right. Regroup if you need to. Remember to add the regrouped number to the product of the next place.

Multiply. Regroup as often as necessary.

1. $\begin{array}{r} 23 \\ \times 4 \\ \hline \end{array}$
2. $\begin{array}{r} 66 \\ \times 3 \\ \hline \end{array}$
3. $\begin{array}{r} 45 \\ \times 5 \\ \hline \end{array}$
4. $\begin{array}{r} 32 \\ \times 8 \\ \hline \end{array}$
5. $\begin{array}{r} 16 \\ \times 7 \\ \hline \end{array}$
6. $\begin{array}{r} 54 \\ \times 9 \\ \hline \end{array}$

7. $\begin{array}{r} 163 \\ \times 5 \\ \hline \end{array}$
8. $\begin{array}{r} 458 \\ \times 7 \\ \hline \end{array}$
9. $\begin{array}{r} 392 \\ \times 6 \\ \hline \end{array}$
10. $\begin{array}{r} 706 \\ \times 8 \\ \hline \end{array}$
11. $\begin{array}{r} 289 \\ \times 4 \\ \hline \end{array}$

12. $\begin{array}{r} \$8.40 \\ \times 3 \\ \hline \end{array}$
13. $\begin{array}{r} \$6.17 \\ \times 9 \\ \hline \end{array}$
14. $\begin{array}{r} \$9.35 \\ \times 2 \\ \hline \end{array}$
15. $\begin{array}{r} \$5.46 \\ \times 6 \\ \hline \end{array}$
16. $\begin{array}{r} \$7.28 \\ \times 5 \\ \hline \end{array}$

17. $\begin{array}{r} 2,746 \\ \times 8 \\ \hline \end{array}$
18. $\begin{array}{r} 9,085 \\ \times 7 \\ \hline \end{array}$
19. $\begin{array}{r} 3,617 \\ \times 3 \\ \hline \end{array}$
20. $\begin{array}{r} 8,263 \\ \times 4 \\ \hline \end{array}$
21. $\begin{array}{r} 7,196 \\ \times 2 \\ \hline \end{array}$

Solve.

22. Giselle earns $5.75 an hour at a flower shop. How much does she earn in an 8-hour day?

23. A dozen long-stemmed roses costs $37.10. Shane sold 5 dozen of them today. How much money did he collect?

24. A trucker drives 4,624 kilometers, round trip, to pick up flowers. How far does he drive if he makes the trip 4 times a month?

25. A local grower raises an average of 35,850 carnations in each of 9 greenhouses. How many carnations are in all 9?

Multiplying by One-Digit Numbers

You can write an equation to help you solve a problem.

Tatsuya is 3 times as old as her little brother. If she is 12, how old is her brother?

Let *n* stand for the number you do not know.

$$3 \times n = 12$$
$$n = 12 \div 3$$
$$n = 4$$

Tatsuya's brother is 4 years old.

Write an equation for each problem. Then solve.

1. In 10 years, Richard will be 21 years old. How old is he now?

2. Andrea's dog is 4 years younger than she is. Her dog is 11. How old is Andrea?

3. Justin's dad is 4 times older than Justin. His dad is 36 years old. How old is Justin?

4. Together, Wanda's grandmother and mother are 100 years old. Wanda's grandmother is 61. How old is Wanda's mother?

5. Gayle's mother was 25 years old when Gayle was born. Her mother is 41 now. How old is Gayle?

6. Just 8 years ago, Floyd was the age his sister is now. If she is 9, how old is Floyd?

7. Mr. Mehta is 9 times older than his youngest grandchild. Mr. Mehta is 63. How old is his youngest grandchild?

8. Herman's uncle is 13 years younger than his pet parrot. The parrot is 50 years old. How old is Herman's uncle?

Problem Solving: Writing an Equation

Division is used to separate a group into smaller groups of equal size. Division is the inverse of multiplication, so you can multiply to check.

quotient → 3 R1
divisor → 3)‾1‾0‾ ← dividend
       9
      1

     3
   × 3
     9
  +1
  10

Divide. Check by multiplying. Remember to add any remainder.

1. 9)‾2‾9‾

2. 2)‾1‾5‾

3. 6)‾4‾2‾

4. 3)‾1‾7‾

5. 8)‾6‾4‾

6. 5)‾2‾3‾

7. 9)‾8‾6‾

8. 4)‾1‾9‾

9. 7)‾5‾5‾

10. 6)‾1‾6‾

11. 3)‾2‾9‾

12. 5)‾3‾4‾

13. 8)‾7‾0‾

14. 7)‾5‾6‾

15. 9)‾7‾5‾

16. 4)‾3‾5‾

17. 9)‾5‾6‾

18. 5)‾4‾1‾

19. 6)‾3‾0‾

20. 8)‾6‾1‾

Division with Remainders

Sometimes a problem has a remainder.

A restaurant chef is planning a lunch for 26 people. If a quart of soup serves 4 people, how many quarts of soup must the chef prepare?

First divide.

$$4 \overline{)26} \quad \begin{array}{r} 6 \text{ R2} \\ \underline{24} \\ 2 \end{array}$$

Now think.

6 quarts serve 24 people. To serve the rest, the chef needs to prepare another quart for a total of 7 quarts of soup.

Solve each problem. Think carefully about the remainder.

1. There are 22 cherry tomatoes in a box. If 3 tomatoes are added to each salad, how many salads can be prepared from one box of tomatoes?

2. The pastry chef has 59 lemons. He uses the juice of 7 lemons in each lemon meringue pie. How many pies can he make? How many lemons will be left?

3. A group of 35 people wants to drive to the Gold Star Restaurant. If 4 people can go in each car, how many cars will the group need?

4. A banquet for 78 people was held. Each table had room for 8 people. What was the smallest number of tables that could be used?

5. The chef has 60 eggs. She needs 8 eggs to make an angel food cake. How many cakes can she make? How many eggs will be left?

6. A beef roast serves 9 people. How many roasts will be needed if the chef is preparing a meal for 30 people?

7. The restaurant kitchen has 42 pounds of peas. If the peas come in 5-pound bags, how many full bags are there? How many pounds remain in the opened bag?

8. Pies are cut into 6 servings. How many pies are needed to serve 40 people?

Divide one place at a time. Divide, multiply, and subtract for each place.

1.
$$
\begin{array}{r}
\times\ 32 \\
3\overline{)96} \\
-9 \\
\hline
6 \\
-6 \\
\hline
\end{array}
$$

2. $4\overline{)48}$

3. $2\overline{)86}$

4. $5\overline{)505}$

5. $3\overline{)630}$

6. $4\overline{)\$7.64}$

7. $6\overline{)\$8.10}$

8. $3\overline{)\$5.58}$

9. $8\overline{)\$9.92}$

Sometimes there are not enough hundreds to divide. Think of the hundreds as tens, for example, 2 hundreds as 20 tens. Be sure to start the quotient in the correct place.

10.
$$
\begin{array}{r}
43 \\
5\overline{)215} \\
-20 \\
\hline
15 \\
-15 \\
\hline
\end{array}
$$

11. $9\overline{)306}$

12. $6\overline{)480}$

13. $2\overline{)194}$

14. $3\overline{)267}$

15. $9\overline{)436}$

16. $7\overline{)367}$

17. $8\overline{)782}$

18. $4\overline{)273}$

19. $5\overline{)380}$

Solve.

20. Kira plans to paint 252 fence posts. She wants to spread the work evenly over 7 days. How many fence posts should she paint each day?

21. Two men painted a 504-foot tower in 8 days. If they painted about the same amount each day, how much did they paint per day?

Dividing by One-Digit Numbers

Divide. Watch for zeros in the quotients.

1.
$$
\begin{array}{r}
807 \\
7\overline{)5{,}649} \\
-56 \\
\hline
4 \\
-0 \\
\hline
49 \\
-49 \\
\hline
\end{array}
$$

2. $4\overline{)2{,}920}$

3. $8\overline{)4{,}112}$

4. $3\overline{)2{,}568}$

5. $2\overline{)\$18.12}$

6. $5\overline{)\$36.90}$

7. $6\overline{)\$28.98}$

8. $9\overline{)\$32.31}$

9. $3\overline{)17{,}202}$

10. $8\overline{)16{,}080}$

11. $5\overline{)40{,}960}$

12. $6\overline{)20{,}850}$

Solve.

13. Bonnie paid $16.14 for 6 rolls of film. What was the price of each roll?

14. Sheldon bought a new camera for $260.00. He paid for it in 8 equal payments. How much was each payment?

Use the table to solve each problem. Be careful—each problem has two or more steps.

★ ★ ★ **STAR PARKING GARAGE** ★ ★ ★

Capacity—452 Cars

First Hour	$1.25
Each additional hour or fraction of an hour	$.75
Maximum 24–hour rate	$8.00
Monthly rate	$75.60

1. At 9 A.M., there were 284 cars in the garage. By noon, 175 more had entered and 91 had left. How many spaces were available at noon?

2. In June, 6,954 cars used the garage. In July, 8,307 cars used it, and in August, 5,175 cars. What was the average number of cars in the garage per month?

3. What is the cost of parking in the garage for 6 hours?

4. Dr. Koch must park in the garage for 9 hours. Which is cheaper, the daily rate or the hourly rate? How much will he save?

5. The garage has 4 floors. Each floor has the same number of spaces except for the top, which has 12 more spaces than the others. How many spaces does each floor have?

6. Mrs. Giordano uses the garage from April through November and pays the monthly rate. How much does she pay for parking per year?

7. Mr. Chan pays the monthly rate. This month, though, he used the garage only 9 days. What was his cost per day? Would he have saved by paying the daily rate?

8. Ms. O'Leary parked her car in the garage from 6 P.M. until 1:30 A.M. What was her total charge?

Problem Solving: Planning Multiple-Step Solutions

Some equations include more than one operation. Do the operations in this order.

1. Work inside parentheses first.
2. Next, multiply and divide from left to right.
3. Finally, add and subtract from left to right.

Solve each equation for *n*.

1. $4 \times (32 - 20) \div 3 + 1 = n$

2. $49 \div 7 + (9 - 4) \times 6 = n$

3. $45 - 36 \div (3 + 3) \times 2 = n$

4. $(51 + 29) \div 4 \times 5 - 3 = n$

5. $(12 - 3) \times (13 + 11) \div 8 = n$

6. $(70 - 28) \div (2 \times 7) + 19 = n$

7. $(72 \div 8) \times (18 + 32) - 200 = n$

8. $7 + 9 \times 6 - 21 \div 3 = n$

Order of Operations

When a number is multiplied by 10, 100, or 1,000, the product is that number with one, two, or three zeros after it.

$$10 \times 8 = 80 \qquad 100 \times 24 = 2,400 \qquad 1,000 \times 36 = 36,000$$

Multiply.

×	1. 6	2. 72	3. 168	4. 302	5. 5,794
10					
100					
1,000					

$$\begin{array}{r} 25 \\ \times 30 \\ \hline 0 \end{array}$$ Think of 30×25 as $3 \times 10 \times 25$. Write one zero; then multiply by 3.

$$\begin{array}{r} 25 \\ \times 300 \\ \hline 00 \end{array}$$ Think of 300×25 as $3 \times 100 \times 25$. Write two zeros; then multiply by 3.

$$\begin{array}{r} 25 \\ \times 3,000 \\ \hline 000 \end{array}$$ Think of $3,000 \times 25$ as $3 \times 1,000 \times 25$. Write three zeros; then multiply by 3.

Multiply.

6. $\begin{array}{r} 38 \\ \times 40 \\ \hline \end{array}$ 7. $\begin{array}{r} 62 \\ \times 70 \\ \hline \end{array}$ 8. $\begin{array}{r} 523 \\ \times 30 \\ \hline \end{array}$ 9. $\begin{array}{r} 852 \\ \times 80 \\ \hline \end{array}$ 10. $\begin{array}{r} 2,571 \\ \times 20 \\ \hline \end{array}$

11. $\begin{array}{r} 18 \\ \times 900 \\ \hline \end{array}$ 12. $\begin{array}{r} 45 \\ \times 500 \\ \hline \end{array}$ 13. $\begin{array}{r} 769 \\ \times 200 \\ \hline \end{array}$ 14. $\begin{array}{r} 284 \\ \times 600 \\ \hline \end{array}$ 15. $\begin{array}{r} 1,302 \\ \times 300 \\ \hline \end{array}$

16. $\begin{array}{r} 22 \\ \times 5,000 \\ \hline \end{array}$ 17. $\begin{array}{r} 69 \\ \times 3,000 \\ \hline \end{array}$ 18. $\begin{array}{r} 175 \\ \times 9,000 \\ \hline \end{array}$ 19. $\begin{array}{r} 807 \\ \times 2,000 \\ \hline \end{array}$ 20. $\begin{array}{r} 3,241 \\ \times 6,000 \\ \hline \end{array}$

Solve.

21. A bookstore ordered 70 copies of a book, which cost $12.95 each. What was the cost of the order?

22. An author received $.82 for each copy of her book that was sold. If 4,000 copies were sold, how much did she receive?

Multiplying by Tens, Hundreds, or Thousands

```
  56
× 34
 224    (4 × 56)
1680    (30 × 56)
1,904   (224 + 1,680)
```

To multiply by a two-digit number, first multiply by the ones. Then multiply by the tens. Finally, add the partial products.

Multiply.

1. 87
   ×54

2. 95
   ×13

3. 45
   ×26

4. 18
   ×47

5. 56
   ×72

6. 48
   ×39

7. 67
   ×62

8. 74
   ×53

9. 57
   ×46

10. 92
    ×85

11. $5.98
    ×35

12. $6.17
    ×91

13. $9.26
    ×48

14. $3.85
    ×67

15. $2.73
    ×82

16. 4,619
    ×27

17. 8,073
    ×75

18. 1,964
    ×54

19. 7,584
    ×19

20. 6,305
    ×38

Solve.

21. In a cross-country road race, Eloise averaged 48 miles an hour. How many miles did she cover if she drove for 24 hours?

22. Anh Thuy earns $18.75 an hour as a mechanic. How much does he earn in 37 hours?

To multiply by larger numbers, multiply by the ones, then by the tens, then by the hundreds, and so on. Then add the partial products.

$$
\begin{array}{r}
419 \\
\times 346 \\
\hline
2514 \\
16760 \\
125700 \\
\hline
144{,}974
\end{array}
$$

(6 × 419)
(40 × 419)
(300 × 419)
(2,514 + 16,760 + 125,700)

Multiply.

1. $\begin{array}{r} 617 \\ \times 193 \end{array}$

2. $\begin{array}{r} 475 \\ \times 364 \end{array}$

3. $\begin{array}{r} 893 \\ \times 290 \end{array}$

4. $\begin{array}{r} 924 \\ \times 586 \end{array}$

5. $\begin{array}{r} 759 \\ \times 816 \end{array}$

6. $\begin{array}{r} 2{,}062 \\ \times 752 \end{array}$

7. $\begin{array}{r} 5{,}900 \\ \times 621 \end{array}$

8. $\begin{array}{r} 3{,}155 \\ \times 905 \end{array}$

9. $\begin{array}{r} 1{,}652 \\ \times 438 \end{array}$

10. $\begin{array}{r} 9{,}213 \\ \times 543 \end{array}$

11. $\begin{array}{r} \$6.12 \\ \times 274 \end{array}$

12. $\begin{array}{r} \$3.78 \\ \times 412 \end{array}$

13. $\begin{array}{r} \$94.60 \\ \times 780 \end{array}$

14. $\begin{array}{r} \$80.41 \\ \times 195 \end{array}$

Solve.

15. The average flying speed of the 747 jet is 936 kilometers an hour. A jet spent 648 hours in the air last year. How many kilometers did it travel?

16. The distance from Seattle to New York is 3,852 kilometers. Captain Lehr has made that trip 115 times. How many kilometers has she traveled on that route?

Multiplying by Three-Digit Numbers

Sometimes a word problem tells you more than you need to know to solve it.

Read each problem carefully and cross out the extra information. Then solve.

1. Aquarium prices range from $2.59 to $535.99. The most popular one sells for $47.50. What is the difference between the cheapest and the most expensive aquarium?

2. Matthew paid $660.75 for a parrot and $325.95 for a cage. He paid for both in 12 monthly payments. How much did he pay for both?

3. The store has 92 zebra fish in stock. 45 of them arrived today. If each sells for $1.56, what is the total value of the zebra fish stock?

4. Nona bought a puppy for $85.34, a leash for $3.72, a collar for $4.99, and a dish for $2.25. How much more did the collar cost than the leash?

5. Winifred works 15 hours a week in the store. She earned $5.15 an hour. Then she got a raise of $.35 an hour. What does she earn now?

6. A case of cat food sells for $25.09. A single can costs $1.25. If the store sold 382 cases this year, how much money did it take in on cases of cat food?

7. Last year, the store sold 632 hamsters. 701 hamsters were sold this year for $3.75 each. How much money did the store take in on hamsters this year?

8. Fish prices range from $.29 to $84.25. An average of 2,378 are sold each month. How many fish are sold in a year?

Estimate products by rounding the factors before multiplying.

$$\begin{array}{r} 520 \\ \times\,29 \\ \hline \end{array}$$

30 times 500 is 15,000. So the answer is about 15,000.

Estimate each product. Then solve and compare the estimated and exact answers.

1.
$$\begin{array}{r} 48 \\ \times\,61 \\ \hline \end{array}$$

2.
$$\begin{array}{r} 198 \\ \times\,39 \\ \hline \end{array}$$

3.
$$\begin{array}{r} 586 \\ \times\,92 \\ \hline \end{array}$$

4.
$$\begin{array}{r} 2,806 \\ \times\,43 \\ \hline \end{array}$$

about

_____

about

_____

about

_____

about

_____

5.
$$\begin{array}{r} 319 \\ \times\,659 \\ \hline \end{array}$$

6.
$$\begin{array}{r} 812 \\ \times\,789 \\ \hline \end{array}$$

7.
$$\begin{array}{r} 6,905 \\ \times\,707 \\ \hline \end{array}$$

8.
$$\begin{array}{r} 5,111 \\ \times\,488 \\ \hline \end{array}$$

about

_____

about

_____

about

_____

about

_____

Greenleaf Nursery raises trees and shrubs that it sells wholesale. Find the estimated and exact costs of each order.

9. 88 lilac bushes at $.49 each

10. 57 holly bushes at $2.15 each

11. 295 dogwood trees at $8.30 each

12. 196 oak trees at $39.95 each

Estimating Products

Dividing by tens is like dividing by ones. Work with as many places in the dividend as you need. Be careful to place the quotient correctly. Multiply and subtract. Then check your work.

Divide.

1. $\dfrac{8}{60 \overline{)480}}$ **Think:** $480 \div 60$
$\underline{480}$

2. $90 \overline{)722}$

3. $50 \overline{)235}$

4. $70 \overline{)354}$

5. $\dfrac{2}{40 \overline{)920}}$ **Think:** $92 \div 40$

6. $80 \overline{)888}$

7. $20 \overline{)738}$

8. $30 \overline{)815}$

9. $\dfrac{7}{60 \overline{)4,380}}$

10. $40 \overline{)3,821}$

11. $20 \overline{)1,786}$

12. $90 \overline{)8,010}$

13. $\dfrac{1}{70 \overline{)7,350}}$

14. $50 \overline{)9,137}$

15. $30 \overline{)9,480}$

16. $20 \overline{)8,740}$

17. $\dfrac{3}{40 \overline{)15,625}}$

18. $80 \overline{)48,640}$

19. $50 \overline{)28,100}$

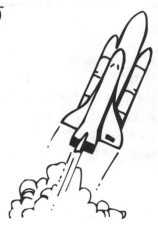

Dividing by Tens

To divide by tens and ones, round the divisor to the nearest ten and estimate the quotient. (Remember, if the digit is 5 or greater, round the number up.) Multiply and subtract. If the estimate is too large or too small, try again. Repeat the steps as necessary.

Divide.

1. $82\overline{)410}$ Think: $410 \div 80$ 2. $38\overline{)250}$ 3. $54\overline{)170}$ 4. $93\overline{)840}$

5. $22\overline{)352}$ 6. $41\overline{)984}$ 7. $65\overline{)2,725}$ 8. $76\overline{)5,776}$

9. $84\overline{)3,192}$ 10. $29\overline{)1,462}$ 11. $47\overline{)3,854}$ 12. $51\overline{)4,692}$

13. $23\overline{)3,000}$ 14. $42\overline{)8,778}$ 15. $71\overline{)30,530}$ 16. $67\overline{)54,203}$

Solve.

17. The Velasco family's electric bill for the month of July was $189.72. What was the average cost per day?

Dividing by Two-Digit Numbers

To divide by a three-digit number, round the divisor to the nearest hundred. Use this rounded number to estimate the quotient at each step of the division. Be careful to place the quotient correctly. Be sure to check your work.

```
              524
    416 ) 217,984     Think: 2179 ÷ 400
          208 0
            9 98       Think: 998 ÷ 400
            8 32
            1 664      Think: 1664 ÷ 400
            1 664
```

Divide.

1. 620) 21,080

2. 480) 34,560

3. 915) 41,175

4. 193) 157,102

5. 657) 190,530

6. 465) 288,300

7. 274) $1,153.54

8. 819) $4,463.55

9. 582) $5,255.46

Solve.

10. Lindsay earned $38,688 last year driving a truck. If she worked 248 days, how much did she earn each day?

11. Lindsay has a load of watermelons worth $505.75. There are 175 watermelons in the load. What is the value of each watermelon?

Dividing by Three-Digit Numbers

Sometimes a word problem does not give you enough information to solve it.

Read each problem carefully and tell what information is needed. Then make up a realistic number or find one in a newspaper. Finally, solve the problem.

1. A special round-trip fare to Denver is $248 for an adult and $186 for a child. How much will it cost Mr. and Mrs. Hendrix and their children to go to Denver?

2. If Roz buys a ticket to Rome before June 30, it will cost only $547 one-way. How much will she save by buying the ticket before rather than after June 30?

3. A luxury cruise in the Mediterranean Sea costs $7,588 per person. What is the cost per person per day?

4. A travel agent sold the luxury cruise to an entire group of people. How much money was collected from the entire group?

5. Mrs. Matsumoto and her 3 children are flying to Tokyo to visit their family. How much will their airfare cost?

6. The Slade family spent a total of $1,155 on a vacation trip to Ocean City, Maryland. On the average, how much did the family spend per day?

7. A cruise to Hawaii costs $1,471. How much cheaper would a flight to Hawaii be?

8. Lorenzo's hotel room costs $69 a night. He also has daily expenses for food and sightseeing. How much does he spend per day, on the average?

Problem Solving: Identifying Insufficient Information

Estimate quotients by rounding the divisor and the dividend before dividing.

$58\overline{)5{,}394}$

58 is about 60 and
5,394 is about 5,400.
5,400 divided by 60 is 90.
So the answer is about 90.

Estimate each quotient. Then solve and compare the estimated and exact answers.

1. $22\overline{)902}$

2. $69\overline{)4{,}347}$

3. $81\overline{)3{,}645}$

4. $529\overline{)24{,}863}$

about

_____

about

_____

about

_____

about

_____

5. $47\overline{)39{,}057}$

6. $71\overline{)50{,}765}$

7. $912\overline{)93{,}024}$

8. $592\overline{)544{,}640}$

about

_____

about

_____

about

_____

about

_____

Below are the quantities and values of some items at Ace Auto Supply. Find the estimated and exact price of each individual item.

9. 58 sparkplugs for $53.94

10. 82 cans of paint for $156.62

11. 179 oil filters for $773.28

12. 287 windshield wiper sets for $2,362.01

The chart below presents some information about Wickey's Widgets, a new business. **Income** is the amount of money taken in from the sale of widgets. **Expenses** are the cost of manufacturing the widgets plus the cost of running the business. **Profit** is what is left of income after the expenses are deducted.

Complete the chart. Then solve each problem below.

Month	Income	Expenses	Profit
January	$33,345	$26,009	
February	$36,270		$8,705
March		$33,345	$10,530
April	$50,025		$14,007
May		$38,029	$16,208
June	$115,500	$77,385	

1. How much profit did the business make from January to June?

2. What was the average monthly income?

3. In January, 57 widgets were sold. What was the selling price of a widget?

4. In June, 210 widgets were sold. What was the selling price then? How does the June price compare to the January price?

5. In April, 96 widgets were made at a cost of $142 each. What was the total cost of making them? How much did the rest of the business expenses amount to?

6. In February, 62 widgets were made for a total cost of $8,370. What was the cost per widget? Did it cost more or less to make than in April?

36

A multiple of a number is the product of that number and any whole number.

Common multiples are the products two numbers share.

The least common multiple (LCM) is the smallest multiple two numbers share.

Multiples
4: 4, 8, 12, 16, 20, 24, . . .
8: 8, 16, 24, 32, 40, 48, . . .

Common Multiples
8, 16, 24, . . .

Least Common Multiple
8

Find each of the following:

		the first ten (or more) multiples	three common multiples	the LCM
1.	2 7			
2.	3 5			
3.	4 10			
4.	6 9			
5.	3 4 8			
6.	6 15			
7.	9 12 18			

Find the least common multiple of each set of numbers.

8. 9, 15

9. 3, 7

10. 4, 6, 9

11. 6, 8

12. 4, 7

13. 5, 6, 8

The factors of a number are the numbers by which it can be divided evenly.
Common factors are the factors two numbers share.
The greatest common factor (GCF) is the largest factor they share.

Factors
12: 1, 2, 3, 4, 6, 12
18: 1, 2, 3, 6, 9, 18

Common Factors
1, 2, 3, 6

Greatest Common Factor
6

Find each of the following:

	Factors	Common Factors	GCF			Factors	Common Factors	GCF
1. 6 8					6. 18 27			
2. 10 15					7. 20 36			
3. 8 12					8. 24 32			
4. 6 15					9. 30 45			
5. 10 14					10. 16 48			

Find the greatest common factor for each set of numbers.

11. 27
    36

12. 28
    40

13. 16
    32

14. 28
    49
    63

15. 36
    45
    54

16. 24
    48
    60

Greatest Common Factor

A prime number, such as 2, has exactly two factors, 1 and itself.

A composite number, such as 4, has more than two factors.

The **prime factorization** of a composite number can be shown on a factor tree.

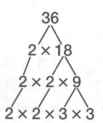

$$36$$
$$2 \times 18$$
$$2 \times 2 \times 9$$
$$2 \times 2 \times 3 \times 3$$

Find all the factors of each number. Then circle each prime number.

1. 2

2. 3

3. 4

4. 5

5. 6

6. 7

7. 8

8. 9

9. 10

Circle each prime number.

11	12	13	14	15	16	17	18	19	20
21	22	23	24	25	26	27	28	29	30
31	32	33	34	35	36	37	38	39	40

Express each composite number as a product of primes using a factor tree.

10. 18

11. 20

12. 27

13. 30

14. 40

15. 50

16. 60

17. 72

A number is divisible by—

2	if the ones digit is an even number. Examples: 30; 3,754; 139,578.
3	if the sum of the digits is divisible by 3. Examples: 12; 114; 103,005.
5	if the ones digit is a 5 or 0. Examples: 95; 3,190; 467,935.
6	if it is divisible by both 2 and 3. Examples: 18; 300; 101,154.
9	if the sum of the digits is divisible by 9. Examples: 27; 936; 265,815.
10	if the ones digit is a 0. Examples: 50; 1,070; 206,730.

Write 2, 3, 5, 6, 9, or 10 beside each number below that is divisible by it.

1. 42

2. 60

3. 93

4. 108

5. 510

6. 882

7. 335

8. 474

9. 711

10. 2,790

11. 4,002

12. 7,135

13. 12,345

14. 36,965

15. 91,058

16. 200,000

17. 611,010

18. 735,104

Solve.

19. Can 171 pine tree seedlings be evenly divided among 9 people?

20. Can 2,364 oak tree seedlings be evenly divided into 6 groups?

Some problems can be solved by guessing the answer and checking the guess against the clues in the problem.

The St. Lawrence River connects the Great Lakes to the Atlantic Ocean. Its length in miles is a three-digit number which is divisible by 2. The sum of its digits is 11. The difference between the ones and tens digits is 1. The ones and hundreds digits are the same. How long is the St. Lawrence River?

The only number that fits *all* the clues is 434. So the river is 434 miles long.

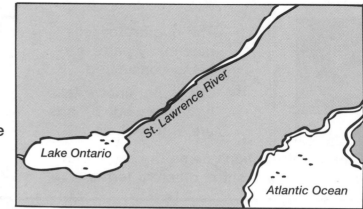

Make a guess and check it to solve each problem.

1. The shallowest of the Great Lakes is Lake Erie. Its greatest depth in feet is a three-digit number that is divisible by 3 and by 10. The sum of its digits is 3. The hundreds digit is twice as large as the tens digit. How deep is Lake Erie?

2. Niagara Falls lies between Lake Erie and Lake Ontario. Its height in feet is a prime number between 100 and 200. The sum of its digits is 14. The difference between the ones and tens digits is 1. How high is Niagara Falls?

3. The widest of the Great Lakes is Huron. Its width in miles is a three-digit number less than 200. It is a multiple of 3 but not of 6. The sum of its digits is 12. The difference between the tens and ones digits is 5. How wide is Lake Huron?

4. The longest of the Great Lakes is Lake Superior. Its length in miles is a three-digit number that is a multiple of 10. The sum of its digits is 8 and the difference is 2. The digit in the hundreds place is larger than the digit in the tens place. How long is Lake Superior?

A fraction has two terms.

$$\frac{3}{4} = \frac{6}{8}$$

The **numerator** tells how many parts are being considered.

The **denominator** tells how many equal parts are in the whole.

Equivalent fractions name the same part of a whole or a set in different terms.

Write fractions to tell what parts are lined, shaded, and plain.

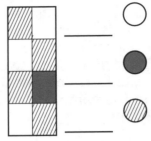

1. _____ _____ _____   ○ ● ◐

2. _____ _____ _____   ○ ● ◐

Write equivalent fractions in higher terms by multiplying both terms by the same number.

3. $\dfrac{2}{3} \times \dfrac{2}{2} = \dfrac{}{6}$ 4. $\dfrac{3}{4} = \dfrac{}{8}$ 5. $\dfrac{1}{6} = \dfrac{}{12}$ 6. $\dfrac{4}{5} = \dfrac{}{10}$ 7. $\dfrac{1}{2} = \dfrac{}{4}$

8. $\dfrac{1}{3} = \dfrac{}{15}$ 9. $\dfrac{4}{9} = \dfrac{}{18}$ 10. $\dfrac{5}{7} = \dfrac{}{28}$ 11. $\dfrac{1}{4} = \dfrac{}{12}$ 12. $\dfrac{7}{8} = \dfrac{}{16}$

Write equivalent fractions in lower terms by dividing both terms by the same number.

13. $\dfrac{8}{12} \div \dfrac{4}{4} = \dfrac{}{3}$ 14. $\dfrac{6}{8} = \dfrac{}{4}$ 15. $\dfrac{4}{10} = \dfrac{}{5}$ 16. $\dfrac{7}{14} = \dfrac{}{2}$ 17. $\dfrac{12}{16} = \dfrac{}{4}$

18. $\dfrac{6}{15} = \dfrac{}{5}$ 19. $\dfrac{12}{18} = \dfrac{}{9}$ 20. $\dfrac{15}{24} = \dfrac{}{8}$ 21. $\dfrac{25}{30} = \dfrac{}{6}$ 22. $\dfrac{6}{21} = \dfrac{}{7}$

Complete each problem with an equivalent fraction.

23. Adam cooked $\dfrac{9}{12}$ of a dozen eggs. He cooked $\dfrac{}{4}$ of the eggs.

24. About $\dfrac{7}{8}$, or $\dfrac{}{24}$, of the Abduls' garden is planted in vegetables.

25. Americans eat $\dfrac{1}{6}$ of their meals away from home. That's $\dfrac{}{30}$ of their meals.

26. Only $\dfrac{8}{24}$ of a case of soda is left. Only $\dfrac{}{3}$ of it is left.

27. Does the hamburger weigh $\dfrac{1}{4}$ pound? Does it weigh $\dfrac{}{16}$ pound?

28. Almost $\dfrac{50}{100}$ of Lana's food budget went for meat. That is $\dfrac{}{2}$ of the food budget.

29. About $\dfrac{2}{3}$, or $\dfrac{}{12}$, of the fish at the store were raised on a farm.

30. Only $\dfrac{3}{21}$ of the cereals contain no added sugar. That's only $\dfrac{}{7}$.

Equivalent Fractions

Fractions are easiest to understand and use when they are in **lowest terms.** A fraction is in **lowest terms,** that is, its simplest form, when it cannot be simplified further.

$$\frac{18}{30} \div \frac{6}{6} = \frac{3}{5}$$

You can find the lowest terms easily by dividing by the greatest common factor (GCF) of the numerator and denominator. For example, the greatest common factor of 18 and 30 is 6.

Write an equivalent fraction in lowest terms.

1. $\frac{8}{12}$ = —   2. $\frac{6}{15}$ = —   3. $\frac{16}{18}$ = —   4. $\frac{24}{30}$ = —   5. $\frac{18}{36}$ = —

6. $\frac{7}{21}$ = —   7. $\frac{9}{36}$ = —   8. $\frac{40}{70}$ = —   9. $\frac{25}{40}$ = —   10. $\frac{9}{54}$ = —

11. $\frac{15}{25}$ = —   12. $\frac{40}{48}$ = —   13. $\frac{8}{28}$ = —   14. $\frac{9}{24}$ = —   15. $\frac{36}{42}$ = —

16. $\frac{15}{30}$ = —   17. $\frac{24}{56}$ = —   18. $\frac{36}{48}$ = —   19. $\frac{10}{18}$ = —   20. $\frac{70}{80}$ = —

21. $\frac{12}{60}$ = —   22. $\frac{30}{42}$ = —   23. $\frac{36}{54}$ = —   24. $\frac{49}{63}$ = —   25. $\frac{20}{75}$ = —

Complete each problem with an equivalent fraction in lowest terms.

26. Clark lives $\frac{6}{10}$ of a mile from the beginning of a trail.

    He lives — of a mile from the trail.

27. North Trail is $\frac{12}{16}$ the length of Crest Trail. It is —

    the length of Crest Trail.

28. The Dengs have hiked $\frac{10}{45}$ of the Appalachian Trail.

    They have hiked — of it.

29. Daisy used $\frac{24}{36}$ of a roll of film on this hike. She used — of it.

30. Ansel drank $\frac{18}{32}$ of a quart of water from his canteen. He drank — of a quart.

To add fractions with common denominators, add the numerators. The denominator stays the same.

Add. Write each sum in lowest terms.

1. $\dfrac{2}{9} + \dfrac{4}{9} = \dfrac{}{9} = \dfrac{}{3}$ 2. $\dfrac{4}{7} + \dfrac{1}{7} =$ 3. $\dfrac{3}{8} + \dfrac{3}{8} =$

4. $\dfrac{1}{12} + \dfrac{7}{12} =$ 5. $\dfrac{1}{10} + \dfrac{3}{10} + \dfrac{4}{10} =$ 6. $\dfrac{7}{16} + \dfrac{5}{16} = \dfrac{2}{16} =$

To add fractions with unlike denominators, first change the fractions to equivalent fractions with common denominators. Use the least common denominator (LCD) to find equivalent fractions. Then add.

Add. Use the least common denominator. Write each sum in lowest terms.

7. $\begin{array}{r} \dfrac{3}{8} = \dfrac{9}{24} \\ + \dfrac{1}{12} = \dfrac{2}{24} \\ \hline \dfrac{11}{24} \end{array}$ 8. $\begin{array}{r} \dfrac{1}{4} \\ + \dfrac{1}{2} \\ \hline \end{array}$ 9. $\begin{array}{r} \dfrac{2}{3} \\ + \dfrac{1}{9} \\ \hline \end{array}$ 10. $\begin{array}{r} \dfrac{3}{10} \\ + \dfrac{1}{5} \\ \hline \end{array}$

11. $\begin{array}{r} \dfrac{1}{3} \\ + \dfrac{5}{12} \\ \hline \end{array}$ 12. $\begin{array}{r} \dfrac{5}{8} \\ + \dfrac{1}{6} \\ \hline \end{array}$ 13. $\begin{array}{r} \dfrac{2}{4} \\ + \dfrac{3}{10} \\ \hline \end{array}$ 14. $\begin{array}{r} \dfrac{2}{6} \\ + \dfrac{5}{9} \\ \hline \end{array}$

15. $\begin{array}{r} \dfrac{4}{7} \\ + \dfrac{1}{4} \\ \hline \end{array}$ 16. $\begin{array}{r} \dfrac{5}{6} \\ + \dfrac{1}{10} \\ \hline \end{array}$ 17. $\begin{array}{r} \dfrac{4}{9} \\ + \dfrac{5}{12} \\ \hline \end{array}$ 18. $\begin{array}{r} \dfrac{1}{5} \\ + \dfrac{5}{8} \\ \hline \end{array}$

19. Owen grew $\dfrac{5}{16}$ of an inch this year and $\dfrac{3}{8}$ of an inch last year. How much did he grow in two years?

20. The family ate $\dfrac{3}{4}$ of a gallon of vanilla ice cream and $\dfrac{1}{6}$ of a gallon of chocolate ice cream. How much was eaten in all?

Adding Fractions

To subtract fractions with common denominators, subtract the numerators. The denominator stays the same.

Subtract. Write each difference in lowest terms.

1. $\dfrac{7}{8} - \dfrac{3}{8} = \dfrac{}{8} = \dfrac{}{2}$

2. $\dfrac{5}{9} - \dfrac{1}{9} =$

3. $\dfrac{9}{12} - \dfrac{1}{12} =$

4. $\dfrac{11}{20} - \dfrac{7}{20} =$

5. $\dfrac{13}{16} - \dfrac{3}{16} =$

6. $\dfrac{17}{24} - \dfrac{5}{24} =$

To subtract fractions with unlike denominators, first change the fractions to equivalent fractions with common denominators. Use the least common denominator (LCD) to find equivalent fractions. Then subtract.

Subtract. Use the least common denominator. Write each difference in lowest terms.

7. $\dfrac{5}{8} = \dfrac{15}{24}$
$-\dfrac{1}{6} = \dfrac{4}{24}$
$\dfrac{11}{24}$

8. $\dfrac{1}{2}$
$-\dfrac{3}{10}$

9. $\dfrac{2}{3}$
$-\dfrac{5}{12}$

10. $\dfrac{3}{4}$
$-\dfrac{3}{16}$

11. $\dfrac{5}{6}$
$-\dfrac{1}{4}$

12. $\dfrac{8}{9}$
$-\dfrac{2}{6}$

13. $\dfrac{3}{4}$
$-\dfrac{1}{10}$

14. $\dfrac{9}{10}$
$-\dfrac{5}{6}$

15. $\dfrac{4}{5}$
$-\dfrac{3}{4}$

16. $\dfrac{6}{7}$
$-\dfrac{1}{3}$

17. $\dfrac{14}{15}$
$-\dfrac{5}{6}$

18. $\dfrac{11}{12}$
$-\dfrac{6}{9}$

19. Jennie wants to loosen a $\dfrac{9}{16}$-inch bolt. Is her $\dfrac{1}{2}$-inch wrench too big or too small? By how much?

20. Dirk must fit a $\dfrac{7}{8}$-inch piece of door trim into a $\dfrac{5}{6}$-inch space. How much must he shave off the door trim?

Read each problem below. Decide which operation or operations you need to solve it. Then write the problem and solve it. Check your answer. Write each answer in lowest terms.

1. For tuna salad, Shawn needs $\frac{2}{3}$ cup sliced celery and $\frac{1}{4}$ cup chopped onion. How many cups of celery and onion are needed?

2. A nut bread recipe calls for $\frac{7}{8}$ cup butter and $\frac{1}{2}$ cup sugar. How much more butter than sugar is needed?

3. A casserole can be baked $\frac{5}{6}$ hour in a regular oven or $\frac{1}{4}$ hour in a microwave oven. How much time does the microwave oven save?

4. Luz melted together $\frac{1}{2}$ pound of cheddar, $\frac{1}{4}$ pound Swiss, and $\frac{1}{8}$ pound jack cheese for a dip. How much cheese did she use?

5. Debra spent $\frac{3}{8}$ of an hour mixing a cake. She then baked it for $\frac{7}{12}$ of an hour. What was the total time from start to finish?

6. Spaghetti sauce cooks for $\frac{11}{12}$ of an hour Spaghetti cooks only $\frac{2}{15}$ of an hour. How long will the sauce cook before Al must start the spaghetti?

7. Chee Kong made $\frac{6}{7}$ of a gallon of ice cream. $\frac{1}{2}$ gallon was eaten then and $\frac{1}{6}$ gallon later. How much was left?

8. There was $\frac{8}{9}$ quart of milk in the refrigerator. Joshua used $\frac{2}{5}$ quart in a recipe and drank $\frac{7}{45}$ quart. How much milk was left?

Problem Solving: Using Fractions

A fraction can name a number equal to a whole number or a mixed number.

To change a fraction to a mixed number, divide the numerator by the denominator. The quotient is the whole number, and the remainder is the numerator of the fraction. The denominator stays the same.

$$\div \frac{13}{4}$$

$$13 \div 4 = 3 \text{ R1}$$

$$\frac{13}{4} = 3\frac{1}{4}$$

Change each fraction to a whole number or a mixed number.

1. $\frac{7}{3} =$ 2. $\frac{20}{4} =$ 3. $\frac{9}{5} =$ 4. $\frac{11}{2} =$

5. $\frac{36}{6} =$ 6. $\frac{21}{8} =$ 7. $\frac{11}{3} =$ 8. $\frac{49}{7} =$

9. $\frac{29}{4} =$ 10. $\frac{25}{12} =$ 11. $\frac{43}{9} =$ 12. $\frac{64}{8} =$

13. Maureen bought $\frac{5}{3}$ (or _____) dozen doughnuts.

14. We walked $\frac{53}{10}$ (or _____) miles in a charity walkathon.

To change a mixed number to a fraction, first multiply the whole number and the denominator. Add the product to the numerator. The sum is the new numerator. The denominator stays the same.

$$+ \ \ 4$$
$$2\frac{4}{5}$$
$$\times$$

$$5 \times 2 = 10$$

$$10 + 4 = 14$$

$$2\frac{4}{5} = \frac{14}{5}$$

Change each mixed number to a fraction.

15. $2\frac{1}{2} =$ 16. $1\frac{2}{3} =$ 17. $4\frac{3}{4} =$ 18. $3\frac{2}{5} =$

19. $1\frac{3}{8} =$ 20. $2\frac{1}{6} =$ 21. $5\frac{1}{3} =$ 22. $4\frac{7}{12} =$

23. $3\frac{7}{9} =$ 24. $5\frac{1}{4} =$ 25. $6\frac{5}{6} =$ 26. $9\frac{1}{7} =$

27. The Enriquez family drinks $3\frac{1}{4}$ (or _____) quarts of milk each day.

28. Benjamin filled the gas tank with $7\frac{4}{5}$ (or _____) gallons of gasoline.

Mixed Numbers and Fractions

To compare fractions with like denominators, compare the numerators.

$$\frac{3}{7} < \frac{4}{7}$$

To compare fractions with unlike denominators, first change them to equivalent fractions with like denominators.

$$\frac{3}{4} > \frac{2}{3} \text{ because } \frac{9}{12} > \frac{8}{12}$$

Compare. Write >, <, or =.

1. $\frac{2}{5} \bigcirc \frac{4}{5}$

2. $\frac{5}{6} \bigcirc \frac{2}{3}$

3. $1\frac{7}{8} \bigcirc 2\frac{1}{8}$

4. $\frac{7}{10} \bigcirc \frac{3}{5}$

5. $\frac{1}{2} \bigcirc \frac{4}{7}$

6. $2\frac{1}{3} \bigcirc 2\frac{1}{2}$

7. $\frac{4}{9} \bigcirc \frac{4}{6}$

8. $\frac{2}{3} \bigcirc \frac{12}{18}$

9. $3\frac{1}{4} \bigcirc 3\frac{1}{5}$

10. $\frac{7}{12} \bigcirc \frac{14}{24}$

11. $\frac{7}{8} \bigcirc \frac{2}{3}$

12. $5\frac{5}{6} \bigcirc 5\frac{22}{24}$

Solve.

13. Mr. Zucca has a $\frac{1}{16}$-inch drill bit and a $\frac{3}{32}$-inch drill bit. Which will make a bigger hole?

14. Mrs. Nichols has a wood screw that is $1\frac{5}{16}$-inches long. If she uses it on a board $1\frac{3}{4}$ inches thick, will the screw come through?

15. It took Adrienne $1\frac{1}{3}$ hours to build a birdhouse and $1\frac{2}{12}$ hours to build a feeder. Which took longer to build?

16. Edward needs a pipe that is $\frac{21}{24}$ of an inch in diameter. The store had only $\frac{7}{8}$-inch pipe. Should he buy it?

Comparing and Ordering Fractions and Mixed Numbers

To add mixed numbers, first change the fractions to equivalent fractions with a common denominator. Then add, first the fractions and then the whole numbers.

Add. Write each sum in lowest terms.

1. $2\frac{1}{10} = 2\frac{2}{20}$
   $+3\frac{3}{4} = 3\frac{15}{20}$
   $\overline{5\frac{17}{20}}$

2. $6\frac{5}{9}$
   $+1\frac{3}{18}$

3. $4\frac{1}{6}$
   $+2\frac{3}{4}$

4. $3\frac{5}{6}$
   $+6\frac{1}{8}$

5. $4\frac{7}{14}$
   $+4\frac{1}{4}$

6. $8\frac{3}{10}$
   $+2\frac{5}{8}$

7. $9\frac{2}{15}$
   $+9\frac{1}{2}$

8. $7\frac{1}{4}$
   $+6\frac{4}{9}$

Sometimes you must regroup a sum in order to write it in lowest terms.

Add. Write each sum in lowest terms.

9. $2\frac{5}{9}$
   $+6\frac{5}{9}$
   $\overline{8\frac{10}{9}} = 9\frac{}{9}$

10. $2\frac{3}{4}$
    $+9\frac{3}{4}$

11. $8\frac{2}{11}$
    $+1\frac{9}{11}$

12. $5\frac{7}{10}$
    $+3\frac{3}{5}$

13. $1\frac{5}{6}$
    $+2\frac{11}{12}$

14. $8\frac{3}{8}$
    $+6\frac{2}{3}$

15. $3\frac{1}{2}$
    $+7\frac{5}{9}$

16. $9\frac{11}{20}$
    $+5\frac{5}{8}$

17. An editor spent $2\frac{1}{2}$ hours in meetings, $4\frac{1}{5}$ hours editing, and $1\frac{3}{10}$ hours checking art. How much time was that in all?

18. A writer spent $4\frac{1}{4}$ hours researching, $10\frac{2}{3}$ hours writing, and $2\frac{5}{6}$ hours typing an article. How much time was that?

To subtract mixed numbers, first change the fractions to equivalent fractions with a common denominator. Then subtract, first the fractions and then the whole numbers.

Subtract. Write each difference in lowest terms.

1. $8\frac{7}{9} = 8\frac{14}{18}$
    $-2\frac{1}{6} = 2\frac{3}{18}$
    $6\frac{11}{18}$

2. $7\frac{7}{10}$
    $-5\frac{3}{10}$

3. $10\frac{3}{8}$
    $-6\frac{1}{4}$

4. $5\frac{5}{6}$
    $-4\frac{3}{4}$

5. $9\frac{2}{3}$
    $-8\frac{2}{5}$

6. $8\frac{7}{8}$
    $-\frac{5}{12}$

7. $28\frac{6}{7}$
    $-14\frac{1}{3}$

8. $18\frac{8}{9}$
    $-6\frac{3}{5}$

Sometimes you must regroup in order to subtract.

Subtract. Write each difference in lowest terms.

9. $6 = 5\frac{7}{7}$
    $-2\frac{4}{7} = 2\frac{4}{7}$
    $3\frac{3}{7}$

10. $8\frac{1}{10} = 7\frac{11}{10}$
    $-3\frac{3}{10}$

11. 17
    $-5\frac{5}{8}$

12. $10\frac{5}{12}$
    $-5\frac{2}{3}$

13. $4\frac{1}{8}$
    $-1\frac{2}{5}$

14. $5\frac{5}{9}$
    $-3\frac{5}{6}$

15. $44\frac{3}{8}$
    $-9\frac{7}{12}$

16. $79\frac{1}{6}$
    $-\frac{9}{10}$

17. A tailor has $5\frac{1}{2}$ yards of cloth. He needs $3\frac{5}{8}$ yards to make a jacket. How much will be left?

18. There are 51 yards of trim on a roll. Mrs. Ono used $24\frac{7}{10}$ yards of it to trim curtains. How much is left?

Subtracting Mixed Numbers

Read each problem below. Decide which operation you need to solve it. Then write the problem and solve it. Check your answer. Write each answer in lowest terms.

1. Mrs. Portnoy used $\frac{7}{8}$ of a liter of paint on the woodwork and $2\frac{1}{6}$ liters on the walls. How much more did she use on the walls?

2. Kam Tai hung $9\frac{1}{5}$ rolls of wallpaper in the living room and $7\frac{1}{2}$ rolls in the dining room. How many rolls did he use in all?

3. Mr. Grove used $16\frac{4}{5}$ meters of fabric to recover a sofa and $4\frac{2}{7}$ meters on a chair. How much fabric did he use on both pieces?

4. Agnes spent $12\frac{2}{3}$ hours stripping paint from an old table and $2\frac{1}{4}$ hours refinishing it. How much less time did it take to refinish?

5. A closet $\frac{5}{6}$ meter deep was built across the end of a room. Before it was built, the room was $7\frac{3}{10}$ meters long. How long is it now?

6. Ms. Flanagan wants to carpet three rooms with areas of $22\frac{2}{5}$, $9\frac{9}{10}$, and $26\frac{4}{15}$ square meters. How much carpeting will she need?

7. A carpenter spent $7\frac{3}{8}$, $2\frac{1}{10}$, $4\frac{7}{10}$, and $\frac{3}{4}$ hours on a job over four visits. What was the total time spent on the job?

8. A picture frame is $70\frac{1}{2}$ centimeters long and $46\frac{2}{3}$ centimeters wide. How much greater is the length than the width?

To find a part of a fraction, multiply the two fractions.

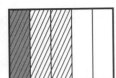
$$\frac{1}{3} \text{ of } \frac{3}{5} = \frac{1}{3} \times \frac{3}{5} = \frac{1 \times 3}{3 \times 5} = \frac{3}{15} = \frac{1}{5}$$

First multiply the numerators.
Then multiply the denominators.

When common factors appear in the numerator and denominator, first divide by the common factor. Then multiply.

$$\frac{2}{3} \times \frac{6}{7} = \frac{2 \times \overset{2}{\cancel{6}}}{\underset{1}{\cancel{3}} \times 7} = \frac{2 \times 2}{1 \times 7} = \frac{4}{7}$$

Multiply. Use the shortcut if possible. Write each product in lowest terms.

1. $\frac{1}{2} \times \frac{8}{9} =$

2. $\frac{3}{4} \times \frac{8}{15} =$

3. $\frac{5}{8} \times \frac{3}{10} =$

4. $\frac{2}{3} \times \frac{9}{11} =$

5. $\frac{9}{10} \times \frac{1}{6} =$

6. $\frac{4}{5} \times \frac{15}{16} =$

7. $\frac{5}{6} \times \frac{18}{25} =$

8. $\frac{3}{4} \times \frac{4}{15} =$

9. $\frac{6}{7} \times \frac{21}{24} =$

10. $\frac{7}{10} \times \frac{5}{28} =$

11. $\frac{4}{9} \times \frac{7}{12} =$

12. $\frac{1}{6} \times \frac{30}{32} =$

13. $\frac{3}{8} \times \frac{16}{21} =$

14. $\frac{11}{12} \times \frac{6}{13} =$

15. $\frac{7}{8} \times \frac{16}{21} =$

16. $\frac{2}{3} \times \frac{15}{22} =$

17. $\frac{3}{4} \times \frac{3}{4} =$

18. $\frac{15}{27} \times \frac{36}{45} =$

19. A bridge span is $\frac{3}{4}$ of a mile long. Workers have repainted $\frac{2}{5}$ of it. How much of it has been repainted?

---

20. The Narrows Bridge is $\frac{2}{3}$ of a mile long. This summer, $\frac{7}{8}$ of it was repaved. How much was repaved?

Multiplying Fractions

To find a fraction of a whole number, think of the whole number as a fraction with a denominator of 1. Multiply the numerators, and then divide by the denominator.

$$\frac{1}{2} \text{ of } 8 = \frac{1}{2} \times \frac{8}{1} = \frac{8}{2} = 4 \qquad\qquad \frac{3}{4} \text{ of } 12 = \frac{3}{\cancel{4}_1} \times \frac{\cancel{12}^3}{1} = \frac{9}{1} = 9$$

Find the number of minutes in each fractional part of an hour.

1. $\frac{1}{2}$ hour = $\frac{1}{2} \times 60$ = _____ minutes

2. $\frac{1}{3}$ hour =

3. $\frac{1}{30}$ hour =

4. $\frac{1}{6}$ hour =

5. $\frac{5}{6}$ hour =

6. $\frac{3}{4}$ hour =

7. $\frac{4}{5}$ hour =

8. $\frac{3}{10}$ hour =

Below are some items on sale at Select Electronics. Find the amount of discount on each item. Then subtract the discount from the regular price to find the sale price.

NOW ON SALE!!	regular price	fractional part off	amount of discount	sale price
9. video cassette	$36	$\frac{1}{4}$		
10. calculator	$15	$\frac{1}{3}$		
11. clock radio	$60	$\frac{2}{5}$		
12. radio/cassette tape player	$96	$\frac{1}{6}$		
13. stereo system	$420	$\frac{1}{10}$		
14. color television	$640	$\frac{3}{8}$		
15. camcorder	$1,200	$\frac{3}{12}$		
16. personal computer	$810	$\frac{2}{9}$		

SALE! VIDEO CASSETTE calculator COLOR TV HOME COMPUTER

To multiply mixed numbers, change the mixed numbers to fractions greater than 1 and multiply.

$$3\frac{1}{3} \times 10\frac{1}{2} = \frac{10}{3} \times \frac{21}{2} = \frac{\cancel{10}^{5}}{\cancel{3}_{1}} \times \frac{\cancel{21}^{7}}{\cancel{2}_{1}} = \frac{5}{1} \times \frac{7}{1} = 35$$

Multiply. Write each product in lowest terms.

1. $2\frac{1}{2} \times 1\frac{1}{3} =$

2. $1\frac{3}{4} \times \frac{4}{7} =$

3. $5\frac{1}{3} \times 1\frac{1}{8} =$

4. $2\frac{2}{3} \times 4\frac{1}{2} =$

5. $1\frac{5}{6} \times \frac{9}{11} =$

6. $27 \times 3\frac{1}{3} =$

7. $\frac{5}{8} \times 3\frac{1}{5} =$

8. $2\frac{4}{7} \times 5\frac{1}{6} =$

9. $2\frac{2}{5} \times 6\frac{2}{3} =$

10. $7 \times 4\frac{6}{7} =$

11. $\frac{5}{9} \times 6\frac{3}{4} =$

12. $2\frac{1}{12} \times 5\frac{1}{3} =$

13. $5\frac{7}{10} \times 5 =$

14. $2\frac{5}{6} \times 3\frac{3}{4} =$

15. $3\frac{1}{2} \times 4\frac{1}{3} =$

16. $2\frac{2}{5} \times 8\frac{5}{6} =$

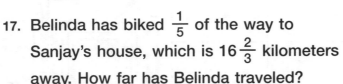

17. Belinda has biked $\frac{1}{5}$ of the way to Sanjay's house, which is $16\frac{2}{3}$ kilometers away. How far has Belinda traveled?

18. Daniel lives $4\frac{1}{5}$ kilometers from one of his grandmothers. His other grandmother lives $7\frac{1}{2}$ times as far away. How far away does this grandmother live?

Multiplying Mixed Numbers

Two factors which have a product of **1** are called **reciprocals** of each other.

$\frac{1}{5}$ and 5 are reciprocals, because $\frac{1}{5} \times \frac{5}{1} = \frac{5}{5} = 1$.

$\frac{2}{3}$ and $\frac{3}{2}$ are reciprocals, because $\frac{2}{3} \times \frac{3}{2} = \frac{6}{6} = 1$.

Write the reciprocal of each number.

1. $\frac{3}{4}$
2. $\frac{2}{5}$
3. $\frac{1}{6}$
4. 3

5. $\frac{5}{3}$
6. $\frac{9}{10}$
7. 12
8. $\frac{1}{7}$

Use a reciprocal to help you divide by a fraction.

Dividing by a fraction is the same as multiplying by its reciprocal.

How many $\frac{1}{3}$ s?

$2 \div \frac{1}{3} = 2 \times \frac{3}{1} = 6$

Divide by multiplying by the reciprocal. Write each answer in lowest terms.

9. $7 \div \frac{1}{2} = 7 \times \underline{\quad} =$

10. $12 \div \frac{3}{4} =$

11. $9 \div \frac{2}{5} =$

12. $5 \div \frac{7}{8} =$

13. $2 \div \frac{8}{9} =$

14. $4 \div \frac{1}{3} =$

15. $6 \div \frac{2}{3} =$

16. $10 \div \frac{4}{5} =$

17. $3 \div \frac{1}{6} =$

18. $8 \div \frac{6}{7} =$

19. $15 \div \frac{1}{4} =$

20. $9 \div \frac{3}{2} =$

21. Timothy baked 5 cakes. If a serving is $\frac{1}{12}$ of a cake, how many servings are there?

22. Flora has 8 cups of sugar. How many pies can she make if she needs $\frac{2}{3}$ cup of sugar for each pie?

To divide a fraction, multiply it by the reciprocal of the divisor.

$$\frac{2}{3} \div \frac{4}{5} = \frac{2}{3} \times \frac{5}{4} = \frac{10}{12} = \frac{5}{6}$$

Divide. Write the answer in lowest terms.

1. $\frac{2}{7} \div \frac{4}{5} = \frac{2}{7} \times \underline{\hspace{1cm}} = \underline{\hspace{1cm}}$

2. $\frac{5}{6} \div \frac{2}{3} =$

3. $\frac{3}{8} \div \frac{9}{4} =$

4. $\frac{2}{5} \div \frac{4}{9} =$

5. $\frac{7}{3} \div \frac{1}{6} =$

6. $\frac{1}{4} \div \frac{2}{5} =$

7. $\frac{2}{3} \div \frac{8}{9} =$

8. $\frac{12}{5} \div \frac{6}{5} =$

9. $\frac{5}{3} \div \frac{10}{7} =$

10. $\frac{3}{8} \div \frac{9}{10} =$

11. $\frac{11}{3} \div 33 =$

12. $\frac{6}{5} \div \frac{2}{15} =$

13. $\frac{3}{4} \div \frac{7}{8} =$

14. $\frac{8}{9} \div 4 =$

15. $\frac{7}{10} \div \frac{1}{5} =$

16. $\frac{6}{7} \div \frac{2}{3} =$

17. $\frac{4}{9} \div \frac{4}{5} =$

18. $\frac{1}{6} \div 5 =$

19. How many hamburgers weighing $\frac{1}{12}$ of a kilogram can Terrence make from $\frac{2}{3}$ of a kilogram of ground beef?

20. Martha needs $\frac{3}{5}$ of a kilogram of butter for a batch of cookies. She has $\frac{9}{10}$ of a kilogram of butter. How many batches can she make?

Dividing Fractions

To divide mixed numbers, first change the mixed numbers to improper fractions. Then divide.

$$11\frac{1}{4} \div 1\frac{1}{2} = \frac{45}{4} \div \frac{3}{2} = \frac{45}{4} \times \frac{2}{3} = \frac{15}{2} = 7\frac{1}{2}$$

Divide. Write each answer in lowest terms.

1. $3\frac{1}{2} \div 1\frac{3}{4} =$

2. $1\frac{3}{5} \div 3\frac{1}{5} =$

3. $1\frac{1}{3} \div \frac{1}{6} =$

4. $10 \div 3\frac{1}{3} =$

5. $1\frac{1}{8} \div 4\frac{1}{2} =$

6. $\frac{3}{7} \div 2\frac{1}{7} =$

7. $2\frac{4}{5} \div 1\frac{3}{4} =$

8. $6\frac{1}{5} \div 2\frac{3}{5} =$

9. $4\frac{3}{4} \div 3\frac{1}{6} =$

10. $2\frac{7}{10} \div 2\frac{5}{8} =$

11. $\frac{5}{16} \div 3\frac{3}{4} =$

12. $4\frac{2}{5} \div 1\frac{1}{10} =$

13. $3\frac{1}{3} \div \frac{6}{7} =$

14. $6\frac{4}{5} \div 4 =$

15. $5\frac{1}{3} \div 1\frac{3}{5} =$

16. $2\frac{2}{3} \div 1\frac{4}{5} =$

17. $10\frac{1}{2} \div 1\frac{1}{6} =$

18. $3 \div 2\frac{5}{8} =$

19. The floor of a room is $17\frac{1}{2}$ feet long. It is covered with tiles $1\frac{1}{4}$ feet long. How many tiles are in one row?

20. A tract of land $50\frac{2}{5}$ acres in size was split into 12 lots of equal size. How big was each lot?

Dividing Mixed Numbers

Read each problem below carefully. Decide which operation is needed to solve it. Then write the problem and solve. Check your answer. Does it make sense?

1. Mrs. Hansen froze $14\frac{1}{3}$ pounds of sweet cherries and $19\frac{4}{5}$ pounds of sour cherries. How many pounds of cherries did she freeze?

2. A dessert recipe calls for $\frac{3}{4}$ cup of sugar. Percy wants to make only $\frac{1}{2}$ the recipe. How much sugar should he use?

3. Chau Wan arranged $18\frac{2}{3}$ pounds of baked ham slices on a tray. If a serving is about $\frac{1}{3}$ pound, how many servings are there?

4. Mr. Ivanoff used $6\frac{1}{5}$ pounds of sausage in a stew. He also used $2\frac{1}{2}$ times as much chicken as sausage. How much chicken did he use?

5. A $24\frac{7}{8}$-pound fish yielded $15\frac{11}{12}$ pounds of meat. How much of the fish was discarded?

6. A roast weighs $11\frac{5}{6}$ pounds. About $\frac{1}{5}$ of it is bone and fat. How much less will it weigh when Ms. O'Hara trims off the bone and fat?

7. Sherman needs $2\frac{2}{3}$ cups of water to make a package of instant rice mix. How much water does he need to make 4 packages of it?

8. A bowl was filled with $9\frac{3}{8}$ quarts of potato salad. If a serving is about $\frac{3}{16}$ of a quart, how many servings are in the bowl?

Problem Solving: Using the Four Operations with Fractions

hundred thousands	ten thousands	thousands	hundreds	tens	ones	decimal point	tenths	hundredths	thousandths	ten thousandths	hundred thousandths
5	1	4	3	6	0	.	8	7	9	5	2

The place values to the right of a decimal point correspond to fractions—tenths, hundredths, thousandths, and so on.

$0.8 = \frac{8}{10}$ $0.87 = \frac{87}{100}$

$0.879 = \frac{879}{1,000}$ $0.8795 = \frac{8,795}{10,000}$

$0.87952 = \frac{87,952}{100,000}$

Write the place value of each underlined digit.

1. 73.4<u>5</u> _____

2. 0.023<u>5</u> _____

3. 0.56<u>8</u> _____

4. 9.6680<u>2</u> _____

5. 1.000<u>7</u> _____

6. 51.<u>0</u>84 _____

7. 4.2<u>9</u>6 _____

8. 2.40<u>1</u>3 _____

9. 2<u>3</u>.72 _____

10. 0.8<u>6</u>92 _____

Write a decimal for each fraction or mixed number.

11. $\frac{82}{100} = $ _____0.82_____

12. $\frac{2}{1,000} = $ _____

13. $18\frac{5}{100} = $ _____

14. $6\frac{6}{10} = $ _____

13. $\frac{546}{1,000} = $ _____

16. $1\frac{75}{1,000} = $ _____

17. $7\frac{7}{100} = $ _____

18. $4\frac{34}{100} = $ _____

19. $8\frac{671}{1,000} = $ _____

20. $\frac{93}{1,000} = $ _____

21. $\frac{106}{1,000} = $ _____

22. $45\frac{99}{1,000} = $ _____

Write a decimal for each number name.

23. twenty-eight hundredths _____

24. thirty-two and fifty-one thousandths _____

25. five hundred and six tenths _____

26. two hundred and two thousandths _____

27. nine and one hundred seventy-three thousandths _____

28. one and seventeen ten-thousandths _____

Decimals: Place Value

Compare decimals by comparing the digits in like places, beginning on the left.

2.457 < 2.458 because 7 thousandths is less than 8 thousandths.

Write >, =, or < to compare each pair of decimals.

1. 2.85 ◯ 2.84   2. 0.232 ◯ 0.322   3. 9.201 ◯ 9.21

4. 7.8 ◯ 8.7   5. 1.001 ◯ 1.010   6. 0.3624 ◯ 3.624

7. 1.90 ◯ 1.89   8. 34.09 ◯ 3.409   9. 7.00001 ◯ 0.70002

10. 4.0 ◯ 0.4   11. 0.025 ◯ 0.24   12. 8.9499 ◯ 9.498

Circle the greatest number in each set. Mark an X on the smallest number.

13. 8.30	14. 6.800	15. 2.9999	16. 1.439
8.03	6.080	3.0000	1.441
8.13	6.008	2.999	1.45

17. 0.9459	18. 4.002	19. 27.099	20. 0.097
0.945	4.0002	27.090	0.906
0.95	3.9992	26.900	0.991

Rank the teams listed below in order of their batting averages, from highest to lowest.

Atlanta .250   New York .267
Chicago .265   Philadelphia .262
Cincinnati .270   Pittsburgh .259
Colorado .282   San Diego .272
Houston .275   San Francisco .253
Los Angeles .264   St. Louis .247

	Team	Batting Average
21.		
22.		
23.		
24.		
25.		
26.		
27.		
28.		
29.		
30.		
31.		
32.		

Comparing and Ordering Decimals

To add decimals, first line up the decimal points. Then add as you do whole numbers.

Rewrite each problem vertically. Then add.

1. 5.02 + 1.9 =

     5.02
   + 1.9

2. 28.63 + 15.47 =

3. 0.509 + 0.32 =

4. 81.635 + 7.39 =

5. 16.0249 + 8.1573 =

6. 4.75 + 2.0896 =

7. 6.4 + 3.008 =

8. 0.52 + 7.603 =

9. 19.8065 + 2.73 =

10. 36.98 + 1.7 + 2.22 =

11. 5.06 + 43 + 0.358 =

12. 9.1 + 0.83 + 1.0955 =

The chart below shows rainfall in inches each month during a recent year in Seattle. Use the information to find the following totals.

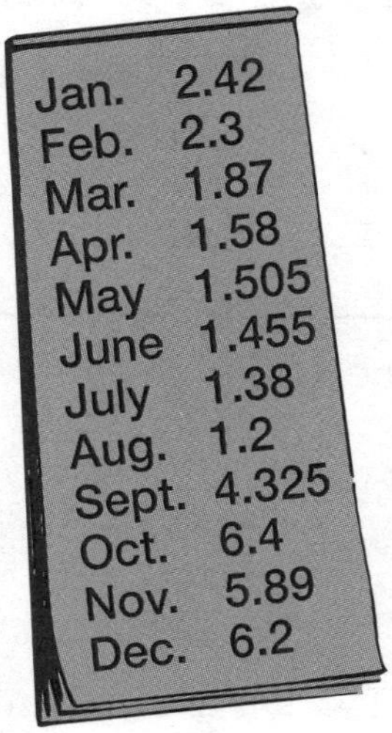

Jan.	2.42
Feb.	2.3
Mar.	1.87
Apr.	1.58
May	1.505
June	1.455
July	1.38
Aug.	1.2
Sept.	4.325
Oct.	6.4
Nov.	5.89
Dec.	6.2

13. rainfall for June, July, and August

14. rainfall for October, November, and December

15. rainfall for the first six months of the year

16. rainfall total for the entire year

Adding Decimals

To subtract decimals, first line up the decimal points. Write zeros if necessary. Then subtract as you do whole numbers.

Rewrite each problem vertically. Then subtract.

1. 35 – 29.7 =

$$
\begin{array}{r}
35.0 \\
-29.7 \\
\hline
\end{array}
$$

2. 4.01 – 1.58 =

3. 78.63 – 9.47 =

4. 0.905 – 0.423 =

5. 61.384 – 7.589 =

6. 8.15 – 0.0743 =

7. 4.95 – 2.9628 =

8. 36.22 – 8.3 =

9. 6.0542 – 0.387 =

10. 9.16 – 1.2905 =

11. 7.4 – 3.009 =

12. 8.52 – 0.611 =

Find the difference between the contents of each pair.

CIDER
1.89 liters

COLA
0.473
liter

MILK
0.237
liter

GRAPE
SODA
0.355
liter

FRUIT
JUICE
1.36 liters

13. cola and cider

14. fruit juice and grape soda

15. fruit juice and cola

16. cider and milk

Subtracting Decimals

Round a number to any place by looking at the next digit on the **right**. If that digit is 4 or less, round **down**. If that digit is 5 or more, round **up**.

Round each number below to the nearest—

		whole number	tenth	hundredth	thousandth
1.	38.1954	38	38.2	38.20	38.195
2.	27.0368				
3.	49.7625				
4.	15.9043				
5.	60.4507				
6.	53.2879				
7.	84.6182				
8.	72.3491				
9.	91.8905				
10.	50.5556				

Very large numbers are sometimes written in a rounded decimal form. This form is easy to understand and is often used in tables and graphs. For example, 40,725,000 can be written as 40.7 million (rounded to the nearest tenth of a million).

Complete this table by writing each number in a decimal form rounded to the nearest tenth of a million.

BUSIEST U.S. AIRPORTS		
Airport	Number of Passengers	Millions in Decimal Form
Chicago (O'Hare)	66,435,252	66.4
Atlanta	54,090,579	
Dallas/Ft. Worth	52,601,125	
Los Angeles	51,050,275	
San Francisco	34,550,652	
Denver	33,129,126	
Miami	30,203,269	
New York (Kennedy)	28,799,275	

Round each decimal to the nearest whole number and estimate the answer. Then find the exact answer and compare it with the estimated answer. *Watch the signs!*

1. 3.21
    +4.82   about ___8___

2. 15.9
    – 7.02   about _____

3. 38.91
    –13.9   about _____

4. 9.063
    –3.14   about _____

5. 6.72
    +6.34   about _____

6. 41.5
    – 9.8   about _____

Round each decimal to the nearest tenth and estimate the answer. Then compare the estimated answer with the exact answer. *Watch the signs!*

7. 2.48
    +0.517   about _____

8. 3.142
    –0.78   about _____

9. 6.95
    +9.98   about _____

10. 8.371
    –0.6   about _____

11. 17.05
    + 4.938 about _____

12. 40.16
    –28.21   about _____

Find the estimated and exact answers for each problem.

13. The tires on Inna's car should be filled to 32 pounds of pressure. One tire is down to 24.7 pounds. How much pressure did it lose?

14. The tank holds 12.5 gallons of gas. Inna filled it with 9.8 gallons. How much was in the tank before she filled it?

15. The odometer on the car reads 8,354.1 miles. If Inna goes on a trip that is 565.8 miles long, what will the odometer read then?

64

Read each problem carefully. Decide which operation you need to solve it. Then solve and check.

1. The winning speed at the first Indianapolis 500 race was 74.59 miles per hour. It had increased by 79.026 miles per hour in 1995. What was the winning speed in 1995?

2. The earth revolves about the sun at 18.5 miles per second. The moon revolves about the earth at 0.63 miles per second. How much faster does the earth revolve?

3. The top running speed of a human is 22.475 miles per hour. The top swimming speed is 5.19 miles per hour. How much faster is the top running speed?

4. A sloth creeps at 0.068 mile an hour on the ground. In the trees, it can improve its speed by 0.102 mile an hour. How fast does it move in the trees?

5. Sound waves travel at 0.2059 mile per second through air. Through steel, the speed is 3.1061 miles per second. How much faster does sound travel through steel?

6. A hummingbird can beat its wings once in 0.011 of a second. A certain bug can beat its wings once in only 0.00045 of a second. How much faster is the bug?

7. In 1992 an Olympic race was won in 43.50 seconds. This race took 10.7 seconds longer the first time it was run, in 1896. What was the winning time of the race in 1896?

8. The fastest mammal, the cheetah, can run 43.4 miles per hour. The fastest bird can fly 106.25 miles an hour. How much greater is the speed of the bird?

To multiply or divide a decimal by 10, 100, or 1,000, move the decimal point one, two, or three places.

To multiply, move the point to the **right**.

8.35 × 10 = 83.5   (one place)

8.35 × 100 = 835.0   (two places)

8.35 × 1,000 = 8,350.0 (three places)

To divide, move the point to the **left**.

29.6 ÷ 10 = 2.96   (one place)

29.6 ÷ 100 = 0.296   (two places)

29.6 ÷ 1,000 = 0.0296 (three places)

Notice that sometimes you must annex zeros to the product or quotient.

Multiply and divide by moving the decimal point. Annex zeros if necessary.

1. 10 × 9.73 =

2. 1,000 × 0.8016 =

3. 502 ÷ 10 =

4. 100 × 1.045 =

5. 168.5 ÷ 100 =

6. 3.2 × 1,000 =

7. 7.08 ÷ 1,000 =

8. 96.2 ÷ 100 =

9. 51.4 × 10 =

10. 130.6 ÷ 1,000 =

11. 3.74 ÷ 10 =

12. 7,088 ÷ 100 =

13. 0.609 × 10 =

14. 0.4 ÷ 100 =

15. 0.008 × 100 =

16. 1,000 × 0.0045 =

17. 0.049 ÷ 10 =

18. 2.367 × 100 =

19. 19.256 ÷ 1,000 =

20. 100 × 9.2 =

Solve.

21. A bakery gave 100 doughnuts worth $35.00 to be sold at a bake sale. How much was each doughnut worth?

22. Mr. Tashiro contributed 100 large brownies that were sold for $.69 each. How much money was made on the brownies?

23. Mrs. Wright figured a pumpkin pie cost $2.03 to make. If she made 10 of them for the bake sale, what did it cost her to make them?

24. To make 1,000 cupcakes, 20.8 pounds of chocolate bits were used. What amount of bits was in each cupcake?

Multiply decimals the same way you multiply whole numbers. The number of decimal places in the product is equal to the sum of the number of decimal places in the factors. Sometimes you must write leading zeros in the product before placing the decimal point.

$$\begin{array}{r} 0.14 \leftarrow 2 \text{ places} \\ \times 0.8 \leftarrow 1 \text{ place} \\ \hline 0.112 \leftarrow 3 \text{ places} \end{array} \qquad \begin{array}{r} 2.8 \leftarrow 1 \text{ place} \\ \times 0.03 \leftarrow 2 \text{ places} \\ \hline 0.084 \leftarrow 3 \text{ places} \end{array}$$

Multiply. Write leading zeros in the product if you need to.

1. $\begin{array}{r} 3.42 \\ \times 6 \\ \hline \end{array}$

2. $\begin{array}{r} 0.92 \\ \times 3.8 \\ \hline \end{array}$

3. $\begin{array}{r} 8.3 \\ \times 27 \\ \hline \end{array}$

4. $\begin{array}{r} 0.25 \\ \times 0.25 \\ \hline \end{array}$

5. $\begin{array}{r} 1.58 \\ \times 4.9 \\ \hline \end{array}$

6. $\begin{array}{r} 1.008 \\ \times 0.05 \\ \hline \end{array}$

7. $\begin{array}{r} 0.637 \\ \times 43 \\ \hline \end{array}$

8. $\begin{array}{r} 0.705 \\ \times 0.65 \\ \hline \end{array}$

9. $\begin{array}{r} 45.7 \\ \times 0.26 \\ \hline \end{array}$

10. $\begin{array}{r} 0.052 \\ \times 0.005 \\ \hline \end{array}$

When multiplying amounts of money by a decimal, round the product to the nearest cent.

Below are some quantity purchases the Juarez family made to stock their freezer. Find the cost of each purchase.

11. 5.75 pounds of chicken at $1.29 a pound $\begin{array}{r} \$1.29 \\ \times 5.75 \\ \hline 7.4175 \\ \text{or } \$7.42 \end{array}$	12. 35.2 pounds of green beans at $.95 a pound	13. 51.8 pounds of pears at $.62 a pound
14. 29.1 pounds of strawberries at $1.53 a pound	15. 8.37 pounds of broccoli at $.78 a pound	16. 89.5 pounds of beef at $2.75 a pound

Multiplying Decimals

To divide a decimal by a whole number, first place a decimal point in the quotient directly above the decimal point in the dividend. Then divide the same way you divide whole numbers. Sometimes you must write leading zeros after the decimal point in the quotient.

$$
\begin{array}{r}
2.4 \\
8\,)\overline{19.2} \\
16 \\
\hline
3\ 2 \\
3\ 2 \\
\end{array}
\qquad
\begin{array}{r}
0.07 \\
25\,)\overline{1.75} \\
1\ 75 \\
\end{array}
$$

Divide. Write leading zeros in the quotient if you need to.

1. $3\,)\overline{28.11}$

2. $7\,)\overline{6.02}$

3. $8\,)\overline{0.344}$

4. $5\,)\overline{7.25}$

5. $49\,)\overline{84.28}$

6. $37\,)\overline{2.405}$

7. $82\,)\overline{171.38}$

8. $91\,)\overline{392.119}$

9. $56\,)\overline{0.504}$

10. $14\,)\overline{1.0248}$

11. $28\,)\overline{0.14}$

12. $65\,)\overline{2.925}$

13. Teresa works as an artist for an advertising agency. She earned $314.84 this week, working 34 hours. What is her hourly wage?

Dividing Decimals by Whole Numbers

To divide a decimal by a decimal, follow these steps to form a simplified problem.

1. Move the decimal point in the divisor to make the divisor a whole number.
2. Move the decimal point in the dividend the same number of places to the right.
3. Place the decimal point in the quotient and divide. Remember to fill in any leading zeros that are needed.

Step 1	Step 2	Step 3
$1.5\overline{)3.75}$	$15\overline{)3.75}$	$15\overline{)37.5}$

Step 3:
$$15\overline{)37.5} \quad \begin{array}{r} 2.5 \\ \underline{30} \\ 7\,5 \\ \underline{7\,5} \end{array}$$

Divide. Remember to place leading zeros where they are needed.

1. $0.6\overline{)3.18}$

2. $0.05\overline{)5.025}$

3. $0.09\overline{)0.0072}$

4. $3.4\overline{)8.84}$

5. $5.2\overline{)9.36}$

6. $0.46\overline{)21.62}$

7. $0.32\overline{)7.104}$

8. $2.9\overline{)0.2755}$

9. $0.008\overline{)0.5136}$

10. $0.023\overline{)1.8653}$

11. $0.104\overline{)0.3432}$

12. $7.98\overline{)127.68}$

13. A chemist used 3.3 bottles of a liquid to get 0.825 of a liter of it. What was the capacity of each bottle?

14. Only 0.05 of a gram of a rare mineral is found in a kilogram of ore. How many kilograms of ore must be refined to get 2.1385 grams of the mineral?

Dividing Decimals by Decimals

Sometimes you must fill in a zero in the dividend when dividing a decimal.

You may need to
write a zero in order
to start dividing.

$$0.15\overline{)1.2\cancel{0}}$$

Or you may need
to write a zero to
continue dividing.

$$\begin{array}{r} 3.46 \\ 25\overline{)86.5\cancel{0}} \\ \underline{75} \\ 11\,5 \\ \underline{10\,0} \\ 1\,5\cancel{0} \\ 1\,5\cancel{0} \end{array}$$

Divide until there is no more remainder. Annex zeros where they are needed.

1. $4\overline{)2.5}$

2. $0.3\overline{)78}$

3. $8\overline{)2.8}$

4. $5\overline{)2}$

5. $3.2\overline{)7.2}$

6. $0.5\overline{)0.44}$

7. $0.82\overline{)12.3}$

8. $78\overline{)35.1}$

9. $65\overline{)119.6}$

10. $0.75\overline{)5.85}$

11. $0.92\overline{)0.874}$

12. $0.024\overline{)16.68}$

13. A 100.8-acre field was subdivided into building lots 1.8 acres in size. How many building lots were made of the field?

14. A particular city block is 5.58 acres large. There are 36 lots on it, all of the same size. What part of an acre is each lot?

Dividing Decimals: Annexing Zeros

Round each decimal to the nearest whole number and estimate the answer. Find the exact answer and compare it with the estimated answer.

1. $\begin{array}{r} 3.9 \\ \times\,3.1 \end{array}$ about _____

2. $\begin{array}{r} 6.3 \\ \times\,0.9\,5 \end{array}$ about _____

3. $\begin{array}{r} 7\,0.1\,4 \\ \times\,2.9 \end{array}$ about _____

4. $1.9\,\overline{)\,87.78}$ about _____

5. $6.8\,\overline{)\,62.56}$ about _____

6. $7.1\,\overline{)\,41.677}$ about _____

Estimation can help you decide if the decimal point is placed correctly in products and quotients.

Use estimation to help you choose each correct answer. Circle the letter.

7. $5.1 \times 3.8 =$
    a. 1.938
    b. 19.38
    c. 193.8

8. $10.7 \times 8.9 =$
    a. 95.23
    b. 9.523
    c. 952.3

9. $0.52 \times 7.6 =$
    a. 395.2
    b. 39.52
    c. 3.952

10. $0.29792 \div 0.98 =$
    a. 3.04
    b. 0.304
    c. 30.4

11. $13.68 \div 7.2 =$
    a. 0.19
    b. 1.9
    c. 19.0

12. $42.054 \div 9.78 =$
    a. 0.43
    b. 43.0
    c. 4.3

Find the estimated and exact answers for each problem.

13. Kathleen drove 129.36 kilometers on 9.8 liters of gas. How many kilometers per liter of gas is that?

14. Hanson filled the tank of his car with 30.1 liters of gas. The cost was $.41 a liter. How much did Hanson pay for the gas?

Estimating Decimal Products and Quotients

Read each problem carefully. Decide which operation or operations you need to solve it. Some problems have more than one step. Solve. Then check your answer.

1. Kwok Lum bought each of his 8 aunts a bottle of perfume. Each bottle held 0.56 of an ounce. How much perfume did he buy altogether?

2. In December, 26.7 inches of snow fell. If 10 inches of snow equals an inch of rain, how much rain would have fallen if it had been warmer?

3. A new candle is 12 inches tall. It burns at a rate of 0.75 inch an hour. How tall will it be after 4.6 hours?

4. Sabrina works 22 hours a week at a burger stand for $113.30. She also wraps gifts at a store for 9.5 hours a week for $56.05. Which job pays more per hour?

5. A company sent 1,000 holiday cards. They cost $.17 each, plus $.06 each for printing the company name. Postage was $.32 each. What was the total cost?

6. A box of 24 Christmas tree ornaments sells for $6.96. A box of 18 similar ornaments sells for $5.58. Which box is the better buy?

7. Mrs. Thorton bought 15.8 yards of pine roping for $.89 a yard and 26.3 yards of ribbon for $.36 a yard. How much did she spend on decorations?

8. Mr. Manfredi bought 4.5 pounds of fancy nuts for $6.90 a pound. The nuts went into 3 cakes of equal size. What was the cost of the nuts per cake?

Problem Solving: Using the Four Operations with Decimals

The abbreviation A.M. is used with times starting at midnight. The abbreviation P.M. is used with times starting at noon.

Solve each problem. Write A.M. or P.M. when the answer is a time of day.

1. The Albas left home at 3:30 A.M. They arrived at Yellowstone National Park at 5:36 P.M. How long did their trip take?

2. It takes 25 minutes for the Albas to set up their tent. If they start at 6:42 P.M., when should they be done?

3. A guided horseback tour starts at 10:12 A.M. and lasts 2 hours and 30 minutes. What time will it be over?

4. The Albas hiked to Inspiration Point. They began their hike at 1:40 P.M. and got to the point at 4:10 P.M. How long did their hike take?

5. Today the sun rose at 5:17 A.M. and set at 8:52 P.M. How long did the daylight last?

6. Old Faithful, a geyser, erupts every 73 minutes on the average. If it last erupted at 11:03 A.M., when could it be expected to erupt again?

7. The Albas went boating on Yellowstone Lake for 2 hours and 50 minutes. If they turned in the boat at 3:20 P.M., what time had they started?

8. A hayride starts at 8:45 P.M. and lasts until 10:15 P.M. How long does it last?

Problem Solving: Finding Elapsed Time

The meter (m) is the basic unit of length in the metric system. A meter is about the distance of a doorknob from the floor.

1,000 meters = 1 kilometer (km)

100 centimeters (cm) = 1 meter

10 millimeters (mm) = 1 centimeter

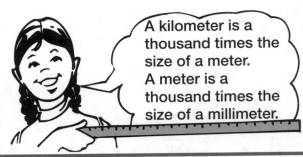

A kilometer is a thousand times the size of a meter. A meter is a thousand times the size of a millimeter.

Write *millimeter*, *centimeter*, *meter*, or *kilometer* to tell which unit you would use to measure the following.

1. the distance between towns _____

2. the height of a bottle _____

3. the width of a road _____

4. the thickness of cardboard _____

5. the length of a hiking trail _____

6. the length of a beetle _____

7. the width of your hand _____

8. the height of a house _____

Metric units are based on 10, so they are easy to convert from one unit to another by multiplying or dividing by 10, 100, 0r 1,000. Remember, you can do that easily by just moving the decimal point right when multiplying and left when dividing. You may need to write in zeros.

Use the table above to help you complete the conversions.

9. 500 m = __0.5__ km

10. 7.5 m = _____ cm

11. 23.8 cm = _____ m

12. 54 mm = _____ cm

13. 8.2 cm = _____ mm

14. 1.5 km = _____ m

15. 6.99 m = _____ cm

16. 7,230 m = _____ km

17. 2.71 cm = _____ mm

18. 9.4 m = _____ mm

19. 807 mm = _____ m

20. 11.9 cm = _____ m

21. Vanessa is 142 centimeters tall. How many meters tall is she? _____

22. Javier jogs 3,560 meters every day for exercise. How many kilometers does he jog? _____

23. Patty noted that 31 millimeters of rain fell in a heavy storm. How many centimeters of rain fell? _____

Solve.

24. Roland walked 6 kilometers in an hour. How many meters did he walk per minute?

74

The milliliter (mL) and liter (L) are basic metric units of capacity.

1,000 millimeters = 1 liter

Complete.

1. 3 liters = _____ milliliters

2. 5 liters = _____ milliliters

3. 0.5 liter = _____ milliliters

4. 100 milliliters = _____ liter

5. 4,075 milliliters = _____ liters

6. 37 milliliters = _____ liter

Write *liter* or *milliliter* to tell which unit you would use to measure the capacity.

7. a washing machine _____

8. a coffee cup _____

9. a picnic jug _____

10. a serving spoon _____

Solve.

11. Orange juice costs $2.80 a liter. Wilma drank 100 milliliters of juice this morning. What did her serving of juice cost?

The gram (g) and kilogram (kg) are basic metric units of mass.

1,000 grams = 1 kilogram

Complete.

12. 6 kilograms = _____ grams

13. 3.78 kilograms = _____ grams

14. 0.9 kilogram = _____ grams

15. 892 grams = _____ kilogram

16. 40 grams = _____ kilogram

17. 1,250 grams = _____ kilograms

Solve.

18. Rufus needs 2 kilograms of corn. It comes in cans that weigh 500 grams and cost $.45 each. How much will the corn cost?

19. The Hagens' dog eats 250 grams of food a day. How many days will a 5-kilogram bag of food last?

Measurement: Metric Units of Capacity and Mass

$$12 \text{ inches (in.)} = 1 \text{ foot (ft)}$$
$$3 \text{ feet} = 1 \text{ yard (yd)}$$
$$5{,}280 \text{ feet} = 1 \text{ mile (mi)}$$

Complete.

1. 1 yard = _____ inches

2. 45 inches = _____ feet and _____ inches

3. 1 mile = _____ yards

4. $2\frac{1}{2}$ miles = _____ yards

5. 12 feet = _____ yards

6. 23 feet = _____ yards and _____ feet

7. 10,560 feet = _____ miles

8. $\frac{3}{4}$ yard = _____ inches

Add or subtract. Regroup when necessary.

9.
```
   2 ft  6 in.
 +3 ft  6 in.
```

10.
```
   6 ft  7 in.
 −1 ft  8 in.
```

11.
```
   4 yd  2 ft  5 in.
 +2 yd  2 ft  7 in.
```

12.
```
   3 yd  2 ft
 +        4 ft
```

13.
```
   7 ft   9 in.
 −       18 in.
```

14.
```
   11 ft  8 in.
    8 ft  7 in.
 +  9 ft  5 in.
```

Solve.

15. Trudy needs 10 feet of curtain fabric for one window and 5 feet for another. How many yards should she buy?

16. Spencer has 4 yards of fake fur. He needs 42 inches for one puppet. How many puppets can he make? How much fur will be left?

17. Mr. Jung used 25 feet of fancy trim on a sofa. It costs $4.59 a yard. How much should Mr. Jung charge for it?

18. A bolt held 11 yards and 2 feet of cloth. A customer bought 7 feet of it. How much was left on the bolt?

19. Olga sewed fringe on 8 curtains. She used 150 inches of it per curtain. How many yards and feet of it did she use?

20. A mile of cloth was used at a factory to make one style of dress. How many dresses were made if each used $1\frac{2}{3}$ yards?

Measurement: Customary Units of Length

2 cups (C) = 1 pint (pt)

2 pints = 1 quart (qt)

4 quarts = 1 gallon (gal)

Complete.

1. 1 quart = _____ cups

2. 18 cups = _____ quarts and _____ pint

3. 1 gallon = _____ pints

4. 50 pints = _____ gallons and _____ quart

5. 4 pints = _____ cups

6. 2 quarts and 1 pint = _____ pints

7. $3\frac{1}{2}$ gallons = _____ quarts

8. 14 cups = _____ pints

9. 15 pints = _____ quarts and _____ pint

Solve.

10. A half-gallon carton of ice cream costs $2.59. A quart costs $1.49. How much is saved by buying the larger package rather than 2 quarts?

11. A gallon of milk costs $2.88. At this rate, what would a pint cost?

16 ounces (oz) = 1 pound (lb)

2,000 pounds = 1 ton

Complete.

12. 4 pounds = _____ ounces

13. 36 ounces = _____ pounds _____ ounces

14. 5 tons = _____ pounds

15. $3\frac{1}{4}$ tons = _____ pounds

16. $2\frac{3}{4}$ pounds = _____ ounces

17. 24 ounces = _____ pounds

18. 1 pound and 10 ounces = _____ ounces

19. 88 ounces = _____ pounds and _____ ounces

Solve.

20. A box of candy weighs 1 pound and 4 ounces. It costs $6.00. What is the cost of the candy per pound?

21. First-class postage is $.32 for the first ounce and $.23 for each additional ounce. How much does it cost to send a package that weighs half a pound?

Some problems contain hidden information.

The heart of a resting person beats an average of 72 times per minute. How many times does it beat in an hour?

You know that there are 60 minutes in an hour. Multiply.

$60 \times 72 = 4{,}320$ beats per hour

Read and solve each problem. Be careful—some problems have more than one step.

1. During exercise, Sharon's heart beats 35 times in 15 seconds. How many times does it beat in 1 minute?

2. Sharon's resting heart rate is 80 beats per minute. How many times does her heart beat in a day?

3. The average adult man masses 72 kilograms. His heart makes up only 312 grams of that amount. How much does the rest of him mass?

4. Signals travel through nerves at up to 100 meters per second. How long does it take a signal to go 1 meter from a fingertip to the brain?

5. The average adult man has 4.7 liters of blood. This amount includes 2.82 liters of plasma, or liquid part. How many milliliters of blood cells make up the rest?

6. A unit of blood equals 450 milliliters. If an average adult man donates 1 unit of blood to the blood bank, how much blood will remain in his body?

7. Each person in a group of 12 donated 1 unit of blood. How many liters did the group donate in all?

8. Hair grows an average of 13 millimeters a month. How many centimeters would it grow in a year?

Problem Solving: Using Hidden Information

A ratio is a comparison of two numbers.
For example, Jeff caught 2 fish with 12 worms.
The ratio of fish to worms is 2 to 12.
The ratio of worms to fish is 12 to 2.

A ratio can also be written with a
colon, 2:12, or as a fraction, $\frac{2}{12}$.

Write the indicated ratio for each set of terms. Use the fractional form.

TERMS	RATIO		TERMS	RATIO
1. 8 girls and 9 boys in a class	girls to boys _____		5. 15 sit-ups in 60 seconds	sit-ups to seconds _____
2. 85 miles in 2 hours	miles to hours _____		6. 15-foot length and 10-foot width	length to width _____
3. 9 lemons for $1.00	lemons to dollars _____		7. $1.05 for 5 cans	cans to dollars _____
4. 2 cups of salt for 5 pounds of ice	cups to pounds _____		8. 3 tables for 12 people	people to tables _____

Equal ratios are like equivalent fractions and are found the same way. Multiply or divide both terms by the same number. For example, to find the number of worms Jeff used per fish, divide: $\frac{12}{2} \div \frac{2}{2} = \frac{6}{1}$, that is, 6 worms for every fish caught.

Complete each chart with equal ratios.

9.

hits	3	6	9	12	15
at bats	10				

10.

cans of beans	4	2	1	6	10
dollars	$1.00				

11.

seeds planted	10	30	20	50	100
seeds sprouted	6				

12.

pages read	2	6	4	10	20
minutes	5				

13.

pushups	8	4	2	6	10
seconds	60				

14.

quarts of soup	2	3	5	10	1
servings	8				

Ratios

A **proportion** is an equation that says that two ratios are equal. Two ratios are equal if their **cross products** are equal.

For example, $\frac{3}{4} = \frac{9}{12}$ is a proportion because $\frac{3}{4} \times \frac{9}{12} \begin{array}{l} = 4 \times 9 = 36 \\ = 3 \times 12 = 36 \end{array}$.

Use cross products to find the missing term in a proportion.

$$\frac{3}{7} = \frac{6}{n}$$

$$3 \times n = 7 \times 6$$

$$3 \times n = 42$$

$$n = 42 \div 3$$

$$n = 14$$

Call the unknown number n.
First multiply to find
the cross products.
Now divide both sides by 3.
The missing term, n, is 14.

Use cross products to solve for n in each proportion.

1. $\frac{1}{4} = \frac{6}{n}$

2. $\frac{2}{6} = \frac{n}{36}$

3. $\frac{9}{5} = \frac{27}{n}$

4. $\frac{8}{n} = \frac{6}{9}$

5. $\frac{n}{5} = \frac{12}{20}$

6. $\frac{2}{7} = \frac{n}{28}$

7. $\frac{6}{30} = \frac{9}{n}$

8. $\frac{n}{7} = \frac{20}{35}$

9. $\frac{9}{n} = \frac{3}{1}$

10. $\frac{4}{n} = \frac{12}{45}$

11. $\frac{5}{8} = \frac{15}{n}$

12. $\frac{3}{2} = \frac{n}{100}$

13. $\frac{8}{6} = \frac{64}{n}$

14. $\frac{15}{4} = \frac{n}{20}$

15. $\frac{n}{10} = \frac{10}{25}$

Some problems can be solved by writing a proportion and finding the missing term.

Jean wants to enlarge a design that is 3 inches wide and 5 inches long. She wants it to be 6 inches wide. How long will the finished design be?

$$\begin{array}{l} \text{width} \\ \text{length} \end{array} \frac{3}{5} = \frac{6}{n}$$

$$3 \times n = 5 \times 6$$
$$3 \times n = 30$$
$$n = 30 \div 3$$
$$n = 10$$

Write a proportion and find the missing term to solve each problem.

1. On Walter's drawing, 2 inches represents 3 feet. The room he drew is actually 12 feet wide. What is its width in the drawing?

2. A costume maker cut 2 costumes from 9 yards of cloth. How much cloth is needed to make 13 costumes?

3. A machine turns out 60 plastic serving trays in 5 minutes. How many does it make in an hour?

4. Rakesh must paint a mural on a wall 8 feet high and 20 feet long. He first drew a sketch 12 inches high. How long was the sketch?

5. Jaqueline can proofread 4 pages in 15 minutes. How long will it take her to proofread 28 pages?

6. A copying machine takes 1.5 minutes to make 10 copies. How long will it take to make 150 copies?

7. A magazine picture was 5 inches wide and 7.5 inches high. The original art was 24 inches high. How wide was the original?

8. Hubert wants to map his garden on a scale of 0.5 inch for a foot. The garden is 25 feet long. Will paper 11 inches long be long enough?

Percent (%) means *per hundred*. Percent is a ratio of some number (*n*) to 100 ($\frac{n}{100}$).
Ratios, fractions, and decimals can be written as percents.
For example, the ratio 1 to 4 can be written as $\frac{1}{4}$ or $\frac{25}{100}$ or 0.25 or 25%.

Write each decimal as a fraction with a denominator of 100 and as a percent.

1. $0.45 = \frac{45}{100} = 45\%$

2. $0.07 =$

3. $0.99 =$

4. $0.6 =$

5. $0.33 =$

6. $0.1 =$

7. $0.56 =$

8. $0.09 =$

9. $0.12 =$

10. Only 0.2 of the students play a musical instrument. _____

11. Violins made up 0.28 of the orchestra. _____

Write each fraction as a percent.

12. $\frac{3}{4} = \frac{75}{100} = 75\%$

13. $\frac{5}{100} =$

14. $\frac{1}{2} =$

15. $\frac{16}{100} =$

16. $\frac{3}{10} =$

17. $\frac{1}{5} =$

18. $\frac{8}{100} =$

19. $\frac{77}{100} =$

20. $\frac{8}{10} =$

21. Mr. Scully's orchard is $\frac{9}{10}$ apple trees. _____

22. About $\frac{3}{5}$ of his apples are the crisp McIntosh kind. _____

Write each percent as a fraction and as a decimal.

23. $29\% = \frac{29}{100} = 0.29$

24. $50\% =$

25. $8\% =$

26. $6\% =$

27. $72\% =$

28. $100\% =$

29. $31\% =$

30. $88\% =$

31. $2\% =$

32. Rain fell on 60% of the days this summer. _____

33. About 85% of our winter storms come from Canada. _____

Fractions, Decimals, and Percents

Chester has $450 in a savings account. The bank pays him 8% interest per year on the account. How much interest will Chester earn on his money in a year?

To find a percent of a number, follow these steps:

1. Write the percent as a decimal. (Or, write it as a fraction if it is easier to work with. For example, 25% can be written as 0.25 or $\frac{1}{4}$.)
2. Multiply.

Step 1	Step 2	
8% = 0.08	$450 × 0.08 ———— $36.00	Chester earned $36.00 interest.

Find the percent of each number below.

1. 76% of 175

2. 25% of 240

3. 66% of $60

4. 9% of 350

5. 81% of 200

6. 50% of 438

7. 17% of 160

8. 20% of 550

9. 45% of 120

Solve.

10. Ms. Weiss has $2,800 of Boffo stock. She received dividends of 5% on the stock last year. What was the total value of the dividends?

11. Stock worth $72.50 per share increased by 2% one day. What was the dollar value of the increase?

12. ZapCo stock was worth $36 a share last year. It is worth 45% more now. How much was the increase? What is a share worth now?

13. Mr. Duong had $18,500 in a retirement fund. Its value rose 12% last year. How much was the increase? How much is in the fund now?

Janice has written 5 of the 8 postcards she bought. What percent has she written?

To find what percent one number is of another number, follow these steps:

1. Write the ratio as a fraction.

2. Divide the numerator by the denominator to change the fraction to a two-place decimal (hundredths). Write a remainder as a fraction in lowest terms.

3. Write the decimal as a percent.

Step 1   Step 2   Step 3

$$\frac{5}{8} = 8\overline{)5.00} \quad 0.62\frac{1}{2} = 62\frac{1}{2}\%$$

$$\begin{array}{r} 4\ 8 \\ \hline 20 \\ 16 \\ \hline \end{array}$$

Janice wrote $62\frac{1}{2}\%$ of the postcards.

Divide to rewrite each fraction as a percent.

1. $\frac{1}{3} =$

2. $\frac{3}{8} =$

3. $\frac{4}{9} =$

4. $\frac{1}{7} =$

5. $\frac{5}{6} =$

6. $\frac{11}{15} =$

Solve.

7. The plane trip to California took 7 hours. Dana slept 3 hours of that time. What percent of the time did she sleep?

8. Winson made a list of 15 things he wanted to see on his trip. He only got to see 9 of them. What percent did he see?

9. Hoa Van identified 15 of the 27 shells she collected on vacation. What percent has she identified?

10. Alvin took 36 photos on his trip. But 5 of them did not come out. What percent did not come out?

Finding a Percent

Connor bought a backpack that was marked 25% off the original price of $45. The sales tax was 6%. What was the total amount Connor paid for the backpack?

Step 1	Step 2	Step 3	Step 4
Multiply to find the amount of discount. (Round to the nearest cent.)	Subtract to find the sale price.	Multiply to find the amount of sales tax. (Round to the nearest cent.)	Add to find the total.

$$\begin{array}{r} \$45 \\ \times\ 0.25 \\ \hline \$11.25 \end{array} \qquad \begin{array}{r} \$45.00 \\ -\ 11.25 \\ \hline \$33.75 \end{array} \qquad \begin{array}{r} \$33.75 \\ \times\ 0.06 \\ \hline \$2.0250 \end{array} \qquad \begin{array}{r} \$33.75 \\ +\ 2.03 \\ \hline \$35.78 \end{array}$$

For each item below, the original price, the percent of discount, and the percent of sales tax are given. Find the—

	amount of discount	sale price	amount of sales tax	total cost
1. poncho was $12.96 now 50% off tax—5%				
2. camp stove was $34.00 now 30% off tax—4%				
3. hiking boots were $65.00 reduced 15% tax—8%				
4. sleeping bag was $87.35 now 25% off tax—3%				
5. tent was $215.00 now 18% less tax—7.5%				

Finding Discount and Sales Tax

Read each problem carefully and decide which operation you need to solve it. Remember—to find what percent one number is of another, divide; to find a percent of a number, multiply. Then solve and check.

1. Mr. Choi left a tip of 15% on a restaurant bill of $32. How much was the tip?

2. Shantay scored 12 points for her team. If her team's final score was 40 points, what percent of the points did Shantay score?

3. Zelma made 36 clay pots. However, 9 of them cracked in the drying oven. What percent of the pots cracked?

4. Nigel saves 60% of the money he earns. How much should he put in the bank if he earned $85 mowing lawns?

5. Priscilla has read 250 pages of a 300-page novel. What percent of the book has she read?

6. Brandon made a 30% down payment on a stereo system that costs $745. How much money did he put down?

7. Ephram plans to print 150 posters. He has 55 of them done. What percent of the posters are done?

8. Mr. and Mrs. Fujiwa want to buy a house that costs $82,900. A down payment of 15% is required. How much money do they need for the down payment?

Problem Solving: Using Percents

Points, lines, line segments, rays, angles, and planes are basic ideas of geometry.

Use the figure on the right to complete each statement.

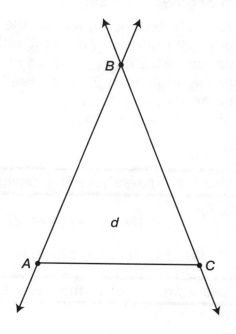

1. $\overleftrightarrow{AB}$ is a _____. It is a straight path with no endpoints.

2. C is a _____. It names a location in space.

3. A _____ is indicated by d. This is a flat surface that extends infinitely in all directions.

4. $\overline{AC}$ is a _____. It is part of a line and has two endpoints.

5. $\overrightarrow{BC}$ is a _____. It is part of a line, has one endpoint, and continues infinitely in the other direction.

6. ∠ABC is an _____. It is made up of two rays that meet at a point called a *vertex*.

Write all the possible names for each figure below.

7.  A   B _____

8.   C   D _____

9.   •E _____

10. G F H _____

11. I J _____

12. K L _____

13. 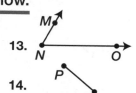 M N O _____

14. P Q _____

15. R S _____

16. T U _____

17. •V _____

18. W X Y _____

Draw the following.

19. ∠ABC   20. $\overleftrightarrow{DE}$ 21. $\overrightarrow{FG}$ 22. ∠HIJ   23. $\overline{KL}$

Angles are measured in units called degrees (°). A protractor is used to measure the number of degrees in an angle.

To use a protractor, line up the arrow or mark on the bottom of it with the vertex of the angle. Line up one ray of the angle with 0°. Then read the number of degrees marked where the other ray passes through.

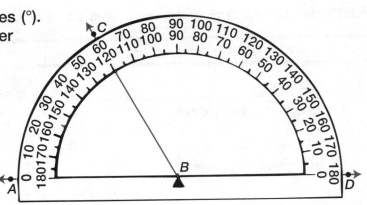

Use the figure above to answer each question.

1. What is the measure of ∠ABC? _____   2. What is the measure of ∠CBD? _____

3. What is the sum of the two measures? _____

Use a protractor to measure each angle. Write the measure inside the angle.

4.

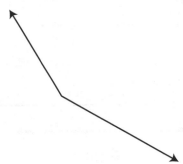

5.

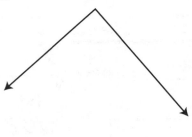

6.

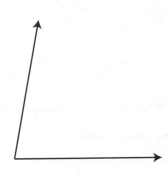

7.

8.

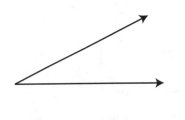

9.

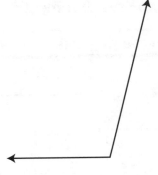

10.

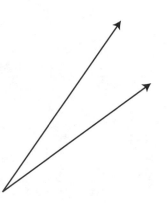

11.

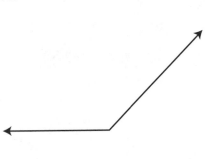

12.

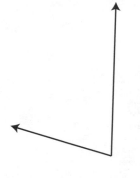

Geometry: Measuring Angles

Angles are classified by their measures.

A straight angle measures 180°.

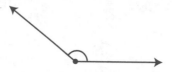

An obtuse angle measures more than 90° but less than 180°.

A right angle measures 90°.

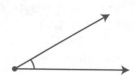

An acute angle measures less than 90°.

Write *straight, obtuse, right,* or *acute* to describe each angle.

1.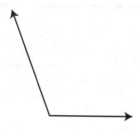

_____

2.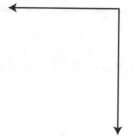

_____

3.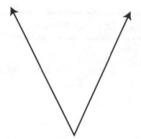

_____

4.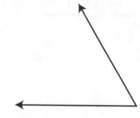

_____

5.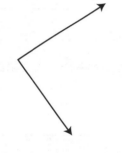

_____

6.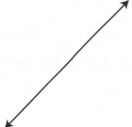

_____

7.

_____

8.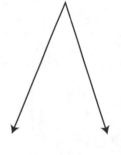

_____

Use the figure below to find the following.

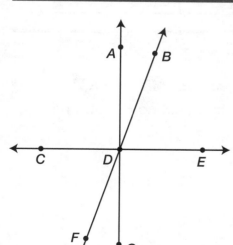

9. Name four right angles. _____

_____

10. Name four acute angles. _____

_____

11. Name three straight angles. _____

_____

12. Name four obtuse angles. _____

_____

Parallel lines never meet. They are always the same distance apart.

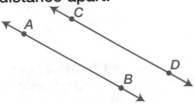

$\overrightarrow{AB}$ is parallel to $\overrightarrow{CD}$.
$\overrightarrow{AB} \parallel \overrightarrow{CD}$

Intersecting lines meet. They form angles.

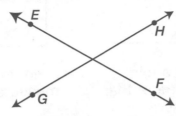

$\overrightarrow{EF}$ intersects $\overrightarrow{GH}$.

Perpendicular lines meet to form right angles.

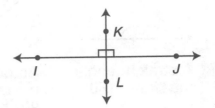

$\overrightarrow{IJ}$ is perpendicular to $\overrightarrow{KL}$.
$\overrightarrow{IJ} \perp \overrightarrow{KL}$

Lines, segments, and rays can be parallel, intersecting, or perpendicular.

Use the figure below to find the following.

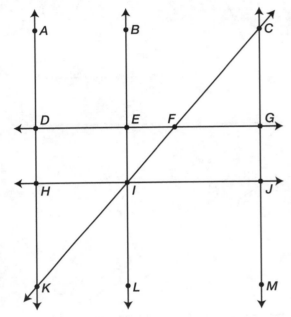

1. Name four pairs of parallel lines. _____

_____

_____

2. Name six pairs of perpendicular lines. _____

_____

_____

3. Name five pairs of lines that intersect but are not

perpendicular. _____

_____

_____

4. Name four angles formed by intersecting lines that are not perpendicular. _____

_____

Draw the following figures.

5. $\overrightarrow{AB} \perp \overrightarrow{CD}$

6. $\overrightarrow{EF} \parallel \overrightarrow{GH}$ and $\overrightarrow{GH} \perp \overrightarrow{IJ}$

7. $\overline{KL} \perp \overline{MN}$ and $\overrightarrow{KM}$
   intersecting $\overleftrightarrow{KL}$ and $\overrightarrow{MN}$

Geometry: Parallel and Intersecting Lines

Triangles are named for the kinds of angles or the number of equal sides they have.

An acute triangle has three acute angles.

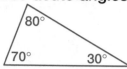

A right triangle has one right angle.

An obtuse triangle has one obtuse angle.

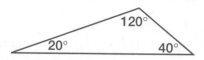

An equilateral triangle has three equal sides.

An isosceles triangle has at least two equal sides.

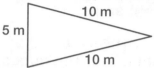

A scalene triangle has no equal sides.

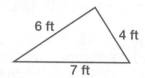

Notice that the sum of the angles always equals 180°.

Use the figure below to find the following.

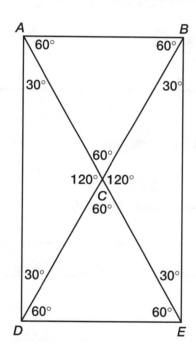

1. Name two acute triangles. _____

2. Name four right triangles. _____

_____

3. Name two obtuse triangles. _____

4. Name two equilateral triangles. _____

5. Name two isosceles triangles. _____

6. Name four scalene triangles. _____

_____

7. In this figure, the _____ triangles are equilateral,

the right triangles are _____, and the isosceles

triangles are _____ .

Find the missing measure in each triangle. Then classify the triangle.

8.

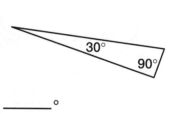

_____°

_____

9.

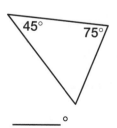

_____°

_____

10.

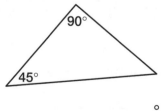

_____°

_____

11.

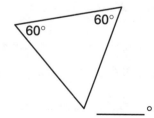

_____°

_____

A quadrilateral is a polygon with four sides. Parallelograms, rectangles, squares, rhombi, and trapezoids are kinds of quadrilaterals.

Use the figures at the right to complete these statements.

1. Figure *ABCD* is a _____. This kind of quadrilateral has opposite sides that are parallel and congruent. The opposite angles are congruent, too.

2. Figure *EFGH* is a _____. This is a kind of parallelogram that has four right angles.

3. Figure *IJKL* is a _____. This is a kind of parallelogram with four congruent sides. The opposite angles are also congruent.

4. Figure *MNOP* is a _____. This is a kind of parallelogram with four congruent sides and four right angles.

5. Figure *QRST* is a _____. This is a kind of quadrilateral with one pair of opposite sides that are parallel.

Answer the following questions.

6. Why are a parallelogram, a rectangle, a square, a rhombus, and a trapezoid all

   quadrilaterals? _____

7. All rectangles are parallelograms, but not all parallelograms are rectangles. Why?

   _____

   _____

8. Can a rhombus be a rectangle? If so, why? _____

   _____

9. Why is a square a parallelogram? _____

   _____

10. Why is a square a rectangle? _____

    _____

11. Why is a square a rhombus? _____

    _____

12. Why is a trapezoid a quadrilateral but not a parallelogram? _____

    _____

Congruent polygons are the same size and shape. The corresponding sides are congruent, and the corresponding angles are equal.

Similar polygons are the same shape but may be different sizes. The corresponding angles are congruent, but the corresponding sides may differ.

  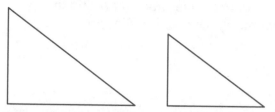

In the figure below, $\overrightarrow{AE} \perp \overleftrightarrow{DG}$ and $\overrightarrow{AG} \parallel \overleftrightarrow{BF} \parallel \overleftrightarrow{DE}$. Use the figure to find the following.

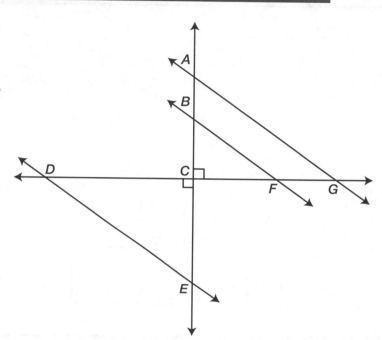

1. Name two congruent triangles.

   _____ and _____

2. Name the corresponding sides of the congruent triangles.

   _____ and _____

   _____ and _____

   _____ and _____

3. Name the corresponding angles.

   _____ and _____

   _____ and _____

   _____ and _____

4. If ∠ACG measures 90°, then ∠ECD measures _____ .

5. If ∠AGC measures 35°, then ∠CAG and ∠CED both measure _____ .

6. If $\overline{DE}$ is 7 inches long, then _____ is also 7 inches long.

7. Name two similar triangles. _____ and _____

8. Name the corresponding sides of the similar triangles.

   _____ and _____

   _____ and _____

   _____ and _____

9. Name the corresponding angles of the similar triangles.

   _____ and _____

   _____ and _____

   _____ and _____

10. If ∠CAG measures 55°, then ∠CBF measures _____ .

11. ∠BFC is congruent to _____ and _____ .

Geometry: Congruent and Similar Polygons

93

A symmetrical figure can be folded along a line of symmetry. The two parts exactly fit each other.

Some figures have more than one line of symmetry. Others have none.

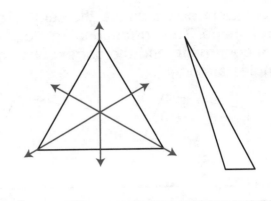

Draw as many lines of symmetry through each figure as possible.

1.

2.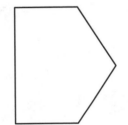

3.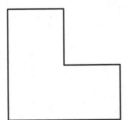

4.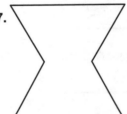

5.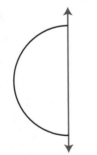

6.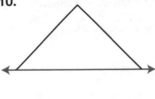

7.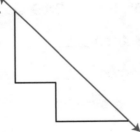

8.

Complete each figure so the line in color is a line of symmetry.

9.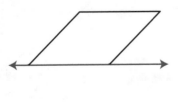

10.

11.

12.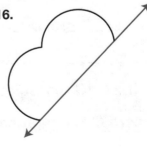

13.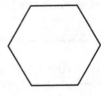

14.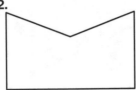

15.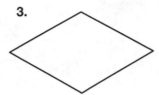

16.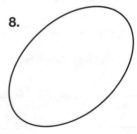

Geometry: Symmetry

The position of a figure can be changed in three ways.

A **translation** is a slide along a straight line.	A **rotation** is a turn around a point.	A **reflection** is a flip on a line of symmetry.
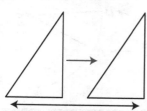	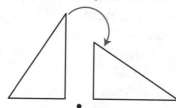	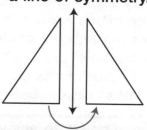

Look at each pair of figures. Then write *translation, rotation,* or *reflection* to describe the kind of change illustrated.

1.

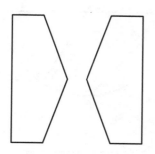

_____

2.

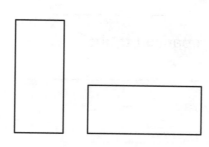

_____

3.

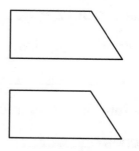

_____

4.

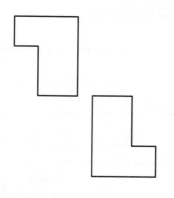

_____

5.

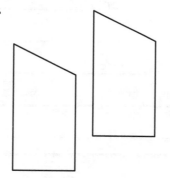

_____

6.

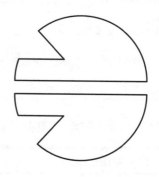

_____

7.

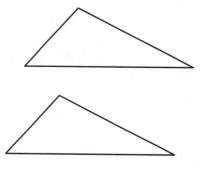

_____

8.

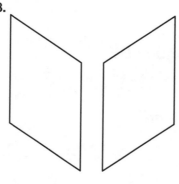

_____

9.

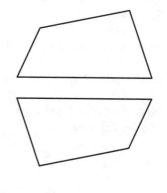

_____

Geometry: Translations, Rotations, and Reflections

A circle is a closed figure. All points on a circle are the same distance from the center.

A radius is a line segment from the center to a point on the circle. A diameter is a line segment that passes through the center and has both endpoints on the circle. A chord is any line segment with both ends on the circle. An arc is any part of the circle between two points.

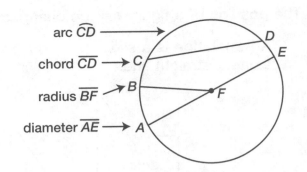

Use the circle below to answer each question.

1. Name the center of the circle. _____

2. Name three radii. _____

3. Name a diameter. _____

4. How long is the diameter in comparison to the

   radius? _____

5. How long is the diameter if the radius is—

   4 inches? _____   9.5 feet? _____   6 miles? _____

6. How long is a radius if the diameter is—

   12 meters? _____   15 centimeters? _____   7.25 kilometers? _____

7. Name four chords. _____

8. A diameter is also a chord. Why? _____

   _____

9. Name five arcs of this circle. _____

Follow the instructions below.

Use a compass to draw a circle with its center on point C. Make the radius 3 centimeters.

Draw two diameters. Label them $\overline{AB}$ and $\overline{DE}$.

Draw two radii. Label them $\overline{CF}$ and $\overline{CG}$.

Draw two chords that are not diameters. Label them $\overline{HI}$ and $\overline{JK}$.

Trace over the arc $\overset{\frown}{AD}$.

•C

Geometry: Circles

The perimeter (P) of a figure is the distance around it. One way to find perimeter is to add the lengths of the sides.

To find the perimeter of a square or rectangle more quickly, multiply.

l = 3 in.

l = 6 in.
w= 3 in.

$P = 4 \times length$

$P = 4 \times 3$

$P = 12$ in.

$P = (2 \times length) + (2 \times width)$

$P = (2 \times 6) + (2 \times 3)$

$P = 18$ in.

Solve each problem. You can draw a picture to help you.

1. A square painting is 48 inches long on a side. How much framing is needed for it?

2. The edges of a rug were sewn with binding. The rug was 2.75 by 4.9 yards in size. How many yards of binding were used on it?

3. A road sign is an equilateral triangle, 60 centimeters long on a side. How much reflecting tape is needed to outline it?

4. A square table has a perimeter of 300 centimeters. What is the length of one side?

5. Lights were strung on the outside of an 8-sided bandstand. Each side was 8 feet long. How many feet of lights were used?

6. The coach outlined a soccer field with a perimeter 330 meters long. The length was 105 meters. How wide was it?

7. Pitkin Park is shaped like a parallelogram. Each long side is 7 miles long. Each short side is 1.8 miles long. What is the perimeter?

Geometry: Perimeter

The circumference (C) of a circle is the distance around it.
To find the circumference, multiply the diameter by π (*pi*).
Pi is a special number that always equals 3.14.

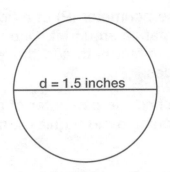

d = 1.5 inches

$$C = 3.14 \times \text{diameter}$$
$$C = 3.14 \times 1.5$$
$$C = 4.71 \text{ in.}$$

Find the circumference of each circle. Be careful—sometimes the radius is given instead of the diameter.

1. d = 2 mi

2. d = 12 m

3. r = 4 in.

4. d = 5.6 cm

5. r = 1.75 ft

6. d = 9.3 km

Solve.

7. Mrs. Lassart sewed lace onto the edge of a round tablecloth that has a diameter of 6 feet. How much lace did she use?

8. Alejandro's bicycle has wheels that are 28 inches in diameter. What is the circumference of one wheel?

9. The distance a wheel travels in one turn is equal to the circumference of the wheel. How far does a wheel 36 centimeters in diameter travel in one turn?

10. Harlan's model plane is flying in circles on a guide wire. If the guide wire is 40 meters long, what is the circumference of the circle the plane is flying in?

Geometry: Circumference

The area (A) of a figure is the number of square units inside it. The square units may be square inches (in.^{2}), square feet (ft^2), square miles (mi^2), and so on.

To find the area of a rectangle or square, multiply the length times the width.

A = length × width
A = 7 × 5
A = 35 ft^2

w = 5 ft

l = 7 ft

The area of a parallelogram is equal to the area of a rectangle with the same base and height.

A = base × height
A = 6 × 5
A = 30 in.^{2}

h = 5 in.

b = 6 in.

Find the area of each figure.

1. a rectangle; l = 9 m, w = 7 m

2. a parallelogram; b = 12 cm, h = 4 cm

3. a rectangle; l = 15 ft, w = 5 ft

4. a parallelogram; b = 10 yd, h = 10 yd

5. a rectangle; l = 25 in., w = 8 in.

6. a parallelogram; b = 100 mi, h = 50 mi

Solve. You can draw a picture to help you.

7. The Mayers built a square deck with an area of 81 square feet. What was the length of a side?

8. A field in the shape of a parallelogram has a base of 500 meters and a height of 100 meters. What is the area of the field?

9. A photograph has an area of 150 square centimeters. If the width is 10 centimeters, what is its length?

10. A can of paint covers 500 square feet. Is it enough to paint a wall that is 8 feet wide and 14 feet long?

The area of a triangle is half the area of a rectangle with the same base and height.

$$A = \frac{1}{2} \times \text{base} \times \text{height}$$

$$A = \frac{1}{2} \times 14 \times 9$$

$$A = \frac{1}{2} \times 126$$

$$A = 63 \text{ in.}^2$$

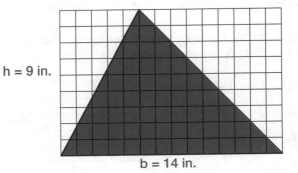

h = 9 in.

b = 14 in.

Find the area of each triangle.

1. b = 7 cm, h = 6 cm

2. b = 8 yd, h = 3 yd

3. b = 12 m, h = 12 m

4. b = 6 ft, h = 22 ft

5. b = 5 km, h = 10

6. b = 42 in., h = 18 in.

Solve. You can draw a picture to help you.

7. A triangular traffic island has a base of 9 feet and a height of 21 feet. What is the area of the traffic island?

8. A triangular pennant has a base of 24 inches and a height of 60 inches. What is the area of the pennant in square feet?

9. A forest fire burned a triangle with a base of 0.8 kilometer and a height of 1.1 kilometers. What was the size of the area destroyed?

10. A tiny city park is a triangle with a base of 80 meters and a height of 120 meters. What is the area of the park?

Geometry: Area of Triangles

The special number π is used to find the area of a circle, as well as the circumference. To find the area, first find the radius and multiply it times itself (radius × radius, <u>not</u> 2 × radius). Then multiply the product by π, 3.14.

$$A = 3.14 \times radius \times radius$$
$$A = 3.14 \times 4 \times 4$$
$$A = 3.14 \times 16$$
$$A = 50.24 \ km^2$$

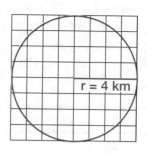

r = 4 km

Remember—the diameter is twice the length of the radius.

Find the area of each circle. Be careful—sometimes the diameter is given instead of the radius.

1. r = 6 in.

2. r = 8 mm

3. r = 5 ft

4. d = 20 m

5. r = 3 mi

6. d = 14 cm

Solve.

7. After a blizzard, Toru built an igloo. The floor was a circle with a radius of 1.5 meters. What was the area of the floor?

8. A fire siren can be heard 9 miles away in all directions. What is the size of the area in which it can be heard?

9. The cut end of a log has a radius of 12 centimeters. What was the area of the cut end?

10. An overhead lamp lights a circle that is 30 meters across. What is the area of the lighted circle?

Some solid geometric figures have only flat surfaces, which are called *faces*.

A prism has two faces called *bases*, which are congruent and parallel polygons. The other faces connect the bases.

A pyramid has one face which is a base. The base may be a polygon of any shape. The other faces all meet at a single vertex.

Use the figures below to complete the following.

A B C   D E F

1. For figures A–C, what polygon are all the faces which are not bases?_____

2. For figures D–F, what polygon are all the faces which are not bases?_____

3. For each figure, tell whether it is a prism or pyramid and name the following.

fig.	prism or pyramid?	base polygon	number of vertices	number of faces	number of edges
A					
B					
C					
D					
E					
F					

Some solid figures, such as cylinders, cones, and spheres, have curved surfaces.

Use the figures below to complete the following.

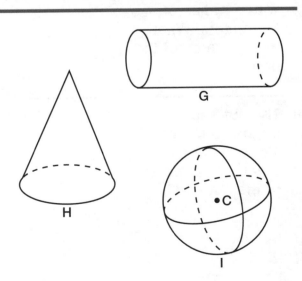

4. Figure G is a _____. It has _____ flat bases which are parallel and congruent. The bases are in the shapes of _____.

5. Figure H is a _____. It has _____ flat base in the shape of a _____.

6. Figure I is a _____. Every point on the figure is the same distance from the center.

The surface (S.A.) of a solid figure is the sum of the areas of its faces.

To find the surface area of a rectangular prism, find the area of each of its six faces. Then add.

Area of—
front = 40 in.²   back = 40 in.²
top = 50 in.²   bottom = 50 in.²
side = 20 in.²   side = 20 in.²

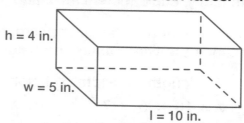

h = 4 in.
w = 5 in.
l = 10 in.

S.A. = 40 + 40 + 50 + 50 + 20 + 20 = 220 in.²

Find the surface area of each object below. Remember to show area in square units.

1.

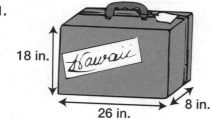

18 in.
26 in.
8 in.

front = _____
back = _____
top = _____
bottom = _____
side = _____
side = _____
S.A. = _____

2.

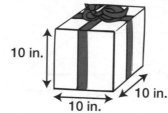

10 in.
10 in.
10 in.

front = _____
back = _____
top = _____
bottom = _____
side = _____
side = _____
S.A. = _____

3.

6 in.
2.5 in.
8 in.

front = _____
back = _____
top = _____
bottom = _____
side = _____
side = _____
S.A. = _____

4.

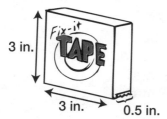

3 in.
3 in.
0.5 in.

front = _____
back = _____
top = _____
bottom = _____
side = _____
side = _____
S.A. = _____

5.

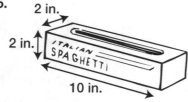

2 in.
2 in.
10 in.

front = _____
back = _____
top = _____
bottom = _____
side = _____
side = _____
S.A. = _____

6.

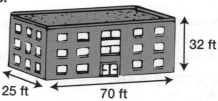

32 ft
25 ft
70 ft

front = _____
back = _____
top = _____
bottom = _____
side = _____
side = _____
S.A. = _____

Geometry: Surface Area

The volume (V) of a solid figure is the number of cubic units inside it. The cubic units may be cubic centimeters (cm^3), cubic meters (m^3), and so on.

To find the volume of a rectangular prism, multiply the length times the width times the height.

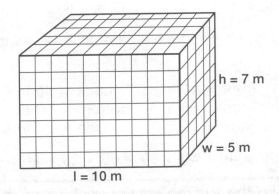

$$V = \text{length} \times \text{width} \times \text{height}$$
$$V = 10 \times 5 \times 7$$
$$V = 350 \ m^3$$

Find the volume of each figure. Remember to write volume in cubic units.

1.
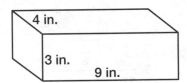
4 in.
3 in.
9 in.

2.
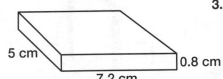
5 cm
0.8 cm
7.2 cm

3.
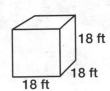
18 ft
18 ft
18 ft

4. l = 100 m, w = 40 m, h = 30 m

5. l = 24 cm, w = 2 cm, h = 6 cm

6. l = 0.7 yd, w = 0.6 yd, h = 1.1 yd

Solve. Each figure is a rectangle prism.

7. While plowing, Gene uncovered a box 22 inches long, 18 inches wide, and 14 inches deep. What was the volume of the box?

8. The feed bin in the barn is 2.8 yards long, 0.75 yards wide, and 1.2 yards high. What is its volume?

9. Hunting fossils, scientists dug a hole 35 meters long, 10 meters wide, and 2.5 meters deep. How many cubic meters of dirt did they remove?

10. Hallie's package had a volume of 10,000 cubic centimeters. It was 20 centimeters high and 10 centimeters wide. How long was it?

Geometry: Volume

$$P = (2 \times l) + (2 \times w) \qquad P = a + b + c \qquad C = 3.14 \times d \qquad V = l \times w \times h$$

$$A = l \times w \qquad A = \frac{1}{2} \times b \times h \qquad A = 3.14 \times r \times r \qquad S.A. = \text{sum of areas of six faces}$$

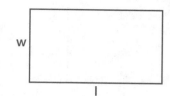 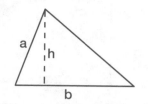 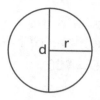 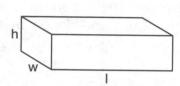

Use the formulas above to solve each problem below.

1. The Olsons' property is a rectangle that is 120 feet wide and 240 feet long. A fence completely encloses it. How long is the fence?

2. What is the area of the Olsons' property?

3. The Olsons poured a square concrete patio. It was 24 feet long on a side and 0.5 foot thick. How many cubic feet of concrete did they use?

4. In the Olsons' yard is a circular fishpond that is 8 feet in diameter. What is the circumference of the fishpond?

5. What is the area of the fishpond?

6. In the Olsons' kitchen is a triangular work island. The base of the triangle is 4 feet and its height is 3 feet. What is the area of the island?

7. The spacious living room is 25 feet long, 16 feet wide, and 14 feet high. What is the volume of this room?

8. What is the surface area of the living room?

Problem Solving: Using Formulas

To find the **range** of a set of data, subtract the lowest number from the highest.

$$31 - 12 = 19$$

To find the **mean**, or average, add the numbers and divide by the number of items.

$$12 + 16 + 31 + 25 + 16 = 100$$
$$100 \div 5 = 20$$

Type of Bread	Number of Loaves Sold
Oat bran	12
Four-grain	16
White	31
Whole wheat	25
Rye	16

To find the **median**, arrange the numbers in order. Then find the number in the middle. If the set has an even number of data, then the median is the mean of the two middle numbers.

$$12 \quad 16 \quad \mathbf{16} \quad 25 \quad 31$$

To find the **mode**, look for the number that occurs most often. A set of data can have one mode, more than one mode, or no mode at all.

Find the range, mean, median, and mode of each set of data.

	Range	Mean	Median	Mode(s)
1. 7, 5, 5, 8, 10				
2. 12, 2, 6, 2, 24, 2				
3. 7, 4, 3, 3, 4, 4, 3				
4. 17, 10, 8, 3, 25, 18, 3				
5. 13, 1, 10, 1, 1, 69, 1, 72				
6. 24, 32, 9, 7, 11, 31, 33, 91, 92				

Solve.

7. Five kinds of bread are priced at $1.84, $1.24, $1.19, $1.37, and $1.46 per loaf. What is the range of the prices?

8. What is the mean price of a loaf of bread?

9. What is the median price of a loaf of bread?

10. What is the mode of the prices?

A double-bar graph compares two sets of data.

Use the double-bar graph to answer the questions.

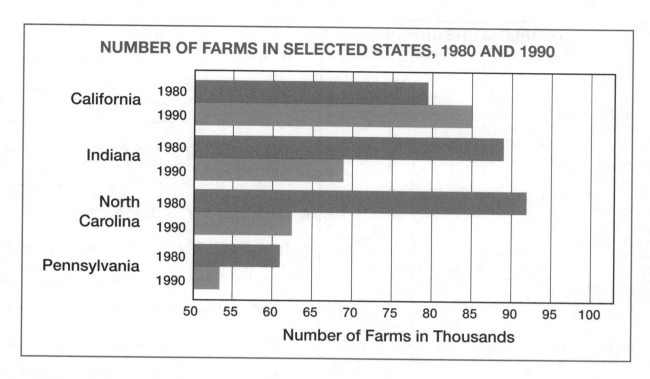

1. What does this graph compare? _____

_____

2. What number does the horizontal scale begin with? _____ What number

does it end with? _____

3. Which state had the most farms in 1980? _____

4. How many farms did it have in 1980? _____ In 1990? _____

5. Did the number of farms increase or decrease? _____

6. Which state had the most farms in 1990? _____

7. Did the number of farms in California increase or decrease from 1980 to 1990?

_____ By about how many? _____

8. In which states did the number of farms decrease from 1980 to 1990? _____

_____

9. Did Indiana or North Carolina have a larger decrease in the number of farms?

_____

10. About how many farms did Pennsylvania lose? _____

A line graph shows change over time.

Use this line graph to answer the questions.

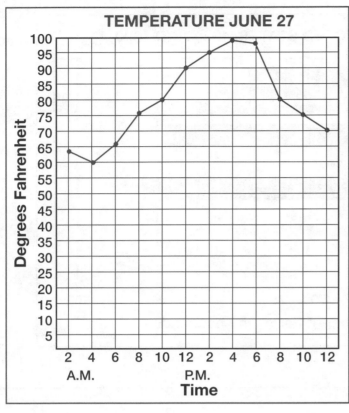

1. What unit was used to record
   temperature? _____

2. How often was it recorded? _____

   _____

3. The sun is highest at noon. Is that the
   hottest time of the day? _____

4. What was the coolest temperature? ____

5. How many degrees did the temperature
   rise that day? _____

6. At what time did the temperature begin
   to fall? _____

7. How many degrees did the temperature
   fall between 6 and 8 P.M.? _____

8. Is the coolest time of the day on this graph just before the sun rose? _____

Humidity is the amount of water in the air. It is written as a percent. When it is high, the air
feels damp. When it is low, the air feels dry. The table below shows daily humidity for two
weeks in September. Use the table to draw a line graph below.

HUMIDITY	
September	%
1	75
2	78
3	85
4	90
5	92
6	90
7	55
8	60
9	65
10	70
11	65
12	75
13	85
14	90

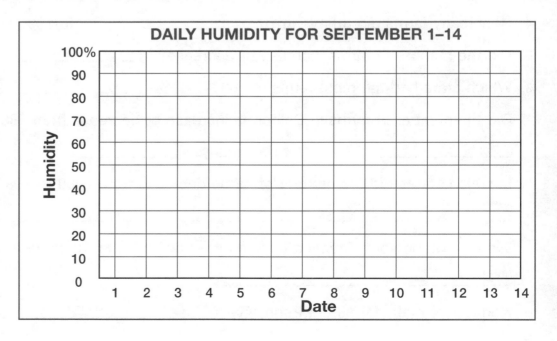

A circle graph shows parts of a whole.

Use the circle graph to answer the questions.

1. What did the Riccis spend the most money on? _____

2. What did they spend the next largest amount on? _____

3. What percent of their income did they spend on these two items? _____

4. Did they spend more on utilities or on car expenses? _____

5. What percent of their income did they save? _____

6. How much more was spent on clothing than was saved? _____

7. What percent was spent on other things and entertainment? _____

MARCH EXPENSES OF THE RICCI FAMILY

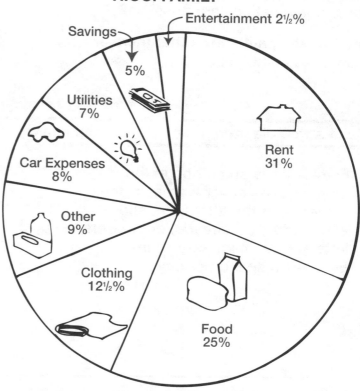

The Riccis' income in March was $2,400. Find how much money was spent on each item. (Hint: Find 31% of $2,400, 25% of $2,400, etc.)

8. rent

9. food

10. clothing

11. other things

12. car expenses

13. utilities

14. savings

15. entertainment

Some problems can be solved by making a tree diagram.

Ahmad has designed a book cover on which the title could be blue or red. The background could be yellow, green, orange, or purple. How many cover combinations are possible?

The tree diagram shows that there are 8 possible combinations.

Title	Background	Combinations
blue	yellow	blue/yellow
	green	blue/green
	orange	blue/orange
	purple	blue/purple
red	yellow	red/yellow
	green	red/green
	orange	red/orange
	purple	red/purple

Make a tree diagram to solve each problem.

1. Esmeralda is an author. In the morning, she either writes or does research. In the afternoon, she either edits, proofreads, or answers letters. How many ways can Esmeralda spend her day?

2. William wants to start an exercise program with two activities. During the week, he could run or bike. On weekends, he could play baseball, basketball, or volleyball. How many possible exercise programs could William set up?

3. Shannon is dressing for work. She could wear a black suit or a white suit. Her blouse could be pink or blue. Her shoes could be black, white, or pink. How many possible outfits could Shannon make?

Probability is the chance of something happening.

Corazón has 3 science fiction books and 4 mysteries. If she picks one at random, what is the probability that it will be a mystery?

$$P(\text{mystery}) = \frac{4}{7} \quad \begin{array}{l}\text{(favorable outcomes)} \\ \text{(possible outcomes)}\end{array}$$

This **probability statement** says that the probability (P) of choosing a mystery is 4 out of 7.

Complete each probability statement.

1. P(black) =

2. P(white) =

3. P(brown) =

4. P(★) =

5. P(■) =

6. P(●) =

7. P(even number) =

8. P(7) =

9. P(prime number) =

Write a probability statement for each problem and solve it.

10. Fu Liang tosses a quarter. What is the probability that it will land heads up?

11. Meredith tosses a die that is numbered from 1 to 6. What is the probability that it will land on 6?

12. On a tray are 3 ham sandwiches and 6 chicken sandwiches. What is the probability of randomly picking a chicken sandwich?

13. In a drawer, Anton has 2 red T-shirts, 3 blue ones, 1 white one, and 2 black ones. What is the probability that he will randomly choose a blue T-shirt?

14. Rowena has 4 $1 bills, 2 $5 bills, and 1 $10 bill. What is the probability that she will randomly pull the $10 bill from her wallet?

15. In a bowl are 5 plums, 4 nectarines, and 6 peaches. What is the probability of picking a peach at random?

Sometimes probability is a fraction equal to 1 or to 0.

The probability that a die numbered from 1 to 6 will land on a number from 1 to 6 is a certainty.

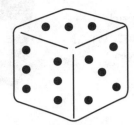

$$P(1 \text{ to } 6) = \frac{6}{6} = 1$$

The probability that a die numbered from 1 to 6 will land on 7 is an impossibility.

$$P(7) = \frac{0}{6} = 0$$

Complete each probability statement.

  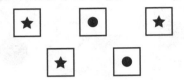

1. P(C) =

2. P(A or B) =

3. P(B) =

4. P(black) =

5. P(black or white) =

6. P(striped) =

7. P(★) =

8. P(■) =

9. P(★ or ●) =

Write a probability statement for each problem and solve it.

10. Desiree's cat had a litter of 5 black kittens. Sariwut was promised one. What is the probability of Sariwut choosing an orange kitten?

11. There are 3 girls and 4 boys on a project committee. If a leader is chosen by pulling a name from a hat, what is the probability that it will be a boy?

12. In a garden are 12 red tulips and 8 yellow ones. What is the probability of randomly picking a tulip that is red or yellow?

13. On a table are 6 dishes of chocolate pudding and 6 dishes of vanilla. What is the probability that Kristi will randomly pick coconut pudding?

14. Orlando has 8 $1 bills in his wallet. What is the probability that he will pull a $1 bill from his wallet?

15. Wrapped in paper inside a packing box are 6 blue mugs, 3 red ones, 2 black, and 1 green one. What is the probability of choosing a yellow mug?

Certainty and Impossibility

To find the combined probability of independent events, multiply the probability of each event.

Clint tossed a penny and a nickel. What is the probability that both coins will land on heads?

Penny	Nickel	Combined
P(heads) = $\frac{1}{2}$	P(heads) = $\frac{1}{2}$	P(heads and heads) = $\frac{1}{2} \times \frac{1}{2} = \frac{1}{4}$

The probability of both coins landing on heads is $\frac{1}{4}$.

Find the probability of each independent event. Then multiply to find the combined probability.

1. Judith has red shorts and blue shorts. She has a white top and a black top. If she puts together an outfit by randomly choosing a pair of shorts and a top, what is the probability that the outfit will include blue shorts and a white top?

2. Soo Youn has white paper, blue paper, and yellow paper. He has pens with black ink, red ink, and blue ink. If he randomly chooses the paper and pen, what is the probability that the letter will be written in black ink on blue paper?

3. Kayla tosses two dice, each numbered from 1 to 6. What is the probability that both dice will land on 6?

Positive numbers and **negative numbers** represent opposites.

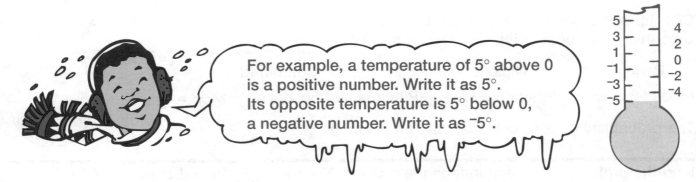

For example, a temperature of 5° above 0 is a positive number. Write it as 5°. Its opposite temperature is 5° below 0, a negative number. Write it as ⁻5°.

Whole numbers and their opposites make up a set of numbers called **integers**. This number line shows integers from ⁻10 (negative ten) to 10 (positive ten). Note that positive numbers may be written without a sign.

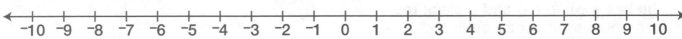

Write the opposite of each integer.

1. 10 _____

2. ⁻4 _____

3. ⁻6 _____

4. 13 _____

5. ⁻9 _____

6. 26 _____

7. 8 _____

8. ⁻45 _____

9. 17 _____

10. ⁻39 _____

11. ⁻3 _____

12. 22 _____

Write an integer for each point described. Use the number line above.

13. 5 units left of 0 _____

14. 2 units right of 0 _____

15. 3 units right of ⁻1 _____

16. 1 unit left of 1 _____

17. 9 units right of ⁻7 _____

18. 6 units left of 3 _____

19. 4 units left of 2 _____

20. 7 units right of ⁻2 _____

Write an integer to describe each situation. Use the number line above.

21. a gain of 6 pounds _____

22. a loss of $25 _____

23. a temperature drop of 5° _____

24. a height of 100 feet _____

25. a football loss of 3 yards _____

26. a tidal rise of 2 feet _____

27. a depth of 500 feet _____

28. a profit of $50 _____

29. a deposit of $20 _____

30. a withdrawal of $35 _____

31. a temperature increase of 7° _____

32. a football gain of 4 yards _____

33. 5 seconds before blast-off _____

34. 10 seconds after blast-off _____

35. income of $1,500 _____

36. expenses of $900 _____

Introduction to Integers

You can compare integers by comparing their positions on a number line. Numbers on the right are greater than numbers on the left.

⁻4 < ⁻2 because ⁻2 is to the right of ⁻4.

5 > ⁻6 because 5 is to the right of ⁻6.

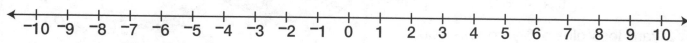

Thinking of a real situation is also helpful. For example, a profit of $6 (6) is greater than a loss of $7 (⁻7).

Write >, <, or = in each circle.

1. 4 ◯ 0

2. ⁻3 ◯ 0

3. ⁻2 ◯ 2

4. 3 ◯ ⁻4

5. ⁻5 ◯ ⁻4

6. ⁻3 ◯ ⁻4

7. 6 ◯ 6

8. ⁻4 ◯ 8

9. ⁻1 ◯ ⁻6

10. 8 ◯ 5

11. ⁻2 ◯ ⁻2

12. ⁻9 ◯ 1

13. ⁻7 ◯ ⁻12

14. ⁻8 ◯ ⁻3

15. 5 ◯ ⁻10

16. 9 ◯ ⁻9

17. ⁻6 ◯ 3

18. ⁻4 ◯ ⁻4

Write the numbers in order from least to greatest.

19. 0, ⁻3, 2 _____

20. ⁻5, ⁻4, ⁻7 _____

21. 7, ⁻4, 2 _____

22. 9, ⁻8, ⁻6 _____

23. ⁻12, 12, 6, ⁻6 _____

24. ⁻2, ⁻4, 1, ⁻21 _____

Write the numbers in order from greatest to least.

25. ⁻5, 5, ⁻8 _____

26. ⁻10, ⁻7, ⁻5 _____

27. ⁻12, ⁻9, 2 _____

28. 3, ⁻15, 20 _____

29. 1, ⁻2, 3, ⁻5 _____

30. ⁻7, 10, ⁻4, 6 _____

Comparing and Ordering Integers

The sum of two positive integers is positive. The sum of two negative integers is negative.

For example, a 5-yard gain plus a 4-yard gain equals a 9-yard gain.

$$5 + 4 = 9$$

A 2-yard loss plus a 6-yard loss equals an 8-yard loss.

$$^-2 + {}^-6 = {}^-8$$

Find each sum.

1. $^-7 + {}^-1 =$ _____

2. $3 + 2 =$ _____

3. $6 + 0 =$ _____

4. $2 + 8 =$ _____

5. $0 + {}^-4 =$ _____

6. $^-9 + {}^-6 =$ _____

7. $^-6 + {}^-6 =$ _____

8. $^-2 + {}^-8 =$ _____

9. $^-10 + {}^-15 =$ _____

You can use a number line to find the sum of a positive integer and a negative integer.

A 3-yard gain plus a 3-yard loss equals 0, that is, no total loss or gain.

$$3 + {}^-3 = 0$$

A gain of 6 yards plus a loss of 4 yards equals a gain of 2 yards.

$$6 + {}^-4 = 2$$

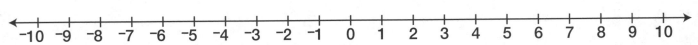

Find each sum. Use the number line above.

10. $^-8 + 3 =$ _____

11. $9 + {}^-6 =$ _____

12. $^-10 + 4 =$ _____

13. $^-5 + 5 =$ _____

14. $^-2 + 5 =$ _____

15. $3 + {}^-12 =$ _____

16. $12 + {}^-5 =$ _____

17. $7 + {}^-16 =$ _____

18. $8 + {}^-8 =$ _____

Solve.

19. The temperature dropped 5° before a storm, and then rose 3° afterwards. What was the total rise or drop?

20. Mr. Santiago wrote a check for $75 this morning. Later he deposited $50 in his checking account. What was the total gain or loss in his account?

Adding Integers

To subtract an integer, add the opposite integer.

On a cold January night, the temperature was 5° above 0 at 8 P.M. By 2 A.M., it had dropped to 2° below 0. How many degrees did the temperature drop in that time?

$$5° - {}^-2° = 5° + 2° = 7°$$

The temperature dropped 7°.

Rewrite each subtraction problem as an equivalent addition problem. Then solve. Use the number line.

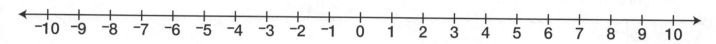

1. $^-7 - 3 =$

2. $6 - {}^-4 =$

3. $^-5 - 8 =$

4. $^-2 - {}^-10 =$

5. $0 - {}^-4 =$

6. $^-8 - 2 =$

7. $0 - 9 =$

8. $5 - {}^-3 =$

9. $^-6 - {}^-1 =$

10. $9 - 4 =$

11. $^-7 - {}^-7 =$

12. $2 - {}^-5 =$

13. $^-8 - {}^-0 =$

14. $^-6 - {}^-5 =$

15. $0 - {}^-3 =$

16. $^-1 - 8 =$

17. $^-4 - {}^-4 =$

18. $7 - {}^-9 =$

Solve.

19. The top of a building is 360 feet above ground level. The basement is 36 feet below ground level. How much higher is the top than the basement?

20. At 2 A.M. the temperature was $^-2°$. By 4 A.M., it had dropped to $^-9°$. How much higher was the temperature at 2 A.M.?

Use the number line to help you solve the problems below.

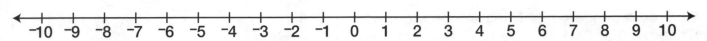

```
←─┼──┼──┼──┼──┼──┼──┼──┼──┼──┼──┼──┼──┼──┼──┼──┼──┼──┼──┼──┼──┼─→
  ⁻10 ⁻9 ⁻8 ⁻7 ⁻6 ⁻5 ⁻4 ⁻3 ⁻2 ⁻1  0  1  2  3  4  5  6  7  8  9  10
```

Find the number which is—

1. 5 more than 1 _____

2. 8 less than 2 _____

3. 2 less than 4 _____

4. 9 more than ⁻9 _____

5. 6 more than ⁻4 _____

6. 3 less than ⁻3 _____

7. 9 more than ⁻5 _____

8. 2 less than ⁻8 _____

Add or subtract.

9. 7 + 2 =

10. ⁻8 + ⁻2 =

11. 13 − ⁻4 =

12. ⁻12 + 4 =

13. 6 − 8 =

14. ⁻1 − ⁻10 =

15. 6 + ⁻7 =

16. ⁻3 − 4 =

17. ⁻7 + ⁻3 =

18. 0 − ⁻5 =

19. 9 + ⁻3 =

20. ⁻8 − 7 =

21. ⁻4 − ⁻6 =

22. 10 − ⁻12 =

23. ⁻8 + ⁻8 =

24. 2 + 5 =

25. 18 − ⁻2 =

26. 5 + ⁻10 =

27. ⁻16 + 8 =

28. ⁻11 + 12 =

29. ⁻4 − 2 =

30. ⁻6 + ⁻6 =

31. ⁻7 − ⁻14 =

32. 20 − 30 =

Solve.

33. Shortly before the sun came up, the temperature was ⁻6°. Within an hour after the sun rose, the temperature shot up 12 degrees. What was the temperature then?

34. The temperature in Garrett's town was 20° above zero. It was ⁻5° at his cousin's home in North Dakota. How many degrees difference is there between the two temperatures?

Adding and Subtracting Integers Practice

Read each problem carefully. Then solve. Think—does the answer make sense?

1. During a dry spell, the water level of a pond dropped to 2 inches below normal. After a heavy rain, the level rose 3 inches. What was the water level then?

2. On February 21, 1918, the temperature in Granville, North Dakota, rose from 33°F below 0 to 50°F above 0. How many degrees did the temperature rise?

3. A share of Wonder Stock rose 4 points on Monday. On Tuesday it fell 6 points. What was its total loss or gain?

4. On Thursday, the price of Wonder Stock rose 3 points a share. Then it fell to 3 points below where it had started. How many points did it fall?

5. On three plays, the football team lost 1 yard, gained 6 yards, and then lost 4 yards. What was the total loss or gain?

6. A hike started at 10 feet below sea level in a valley and ended 75 feet above sea level on a hill. How much higher is the ending place than the starting place?

7. A diver was swimming at a depth of 10 feet. She swam down another 30 feet. How far under the surface of the water is she now?

Problem Solving: Using Integers

An ordered pair of integers, or coordinates, names the location of a point on a grid. The first integer tells how many units right or left the point is. The second integer tells how many units up or down it is.

(⁻2,5) names a point that is 2 units to the left and 5 units up.

Name the directions and coordinates for each point.

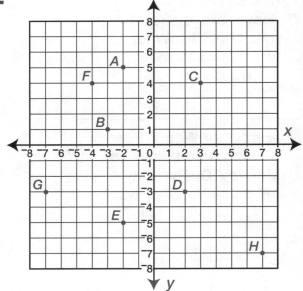

Point	Directions		Coordinates
1. A	left 2	up 5	(⁻2,5)
2. B	_____	_____	( )
3. C	_____	_____	( )
4. D	_____	_____	( )
5. E	_____	_____	( )
6. F	_____	_____	( )
7. G	_____	_____	( )
8. H	_____	_____	( )

Name the point for each ordered pair.

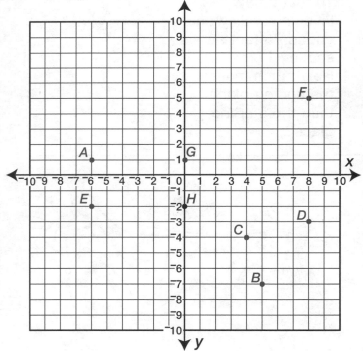

9. (⁻6,⁻2) _____   10. (5,⁻7) _____

11. (⁻6, 1) _____   12. (8, 5) _____

13. (0, 1) _____   14. (8, ⁻3) _____

15. (4, ⁻4) _____   16. (0, ⁻2) _____

Graph and label these points:

A (0,9)	B (6,2)	C (0,2)
D (⁻5,2)	E (⁻6,1)	F (0,1)
G (9,1)	H (7,⁻1)	I (⁻4,⁻1)

Then draw these line segments:

$\overline{AB}$, $\overline{AD}$, $\overline{BD}$, $\overline{CF}$, $\overline{EG}$, $\overline{EI}$, $\overline{IH}$, $\overline{GH}$

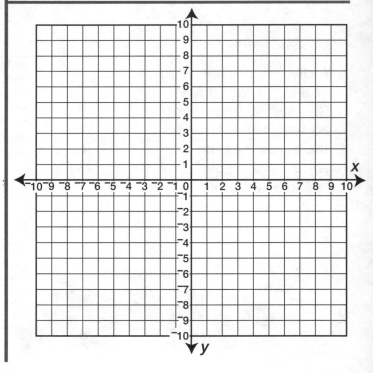

Ordered Pairs